Dissonant Methods

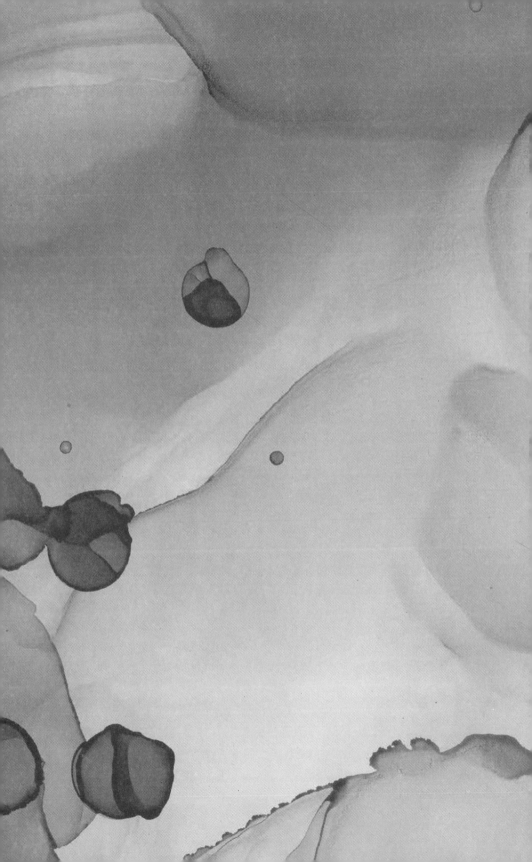

ADA S. JAARSMA
& KIT DOBSON

Editors

Undoing Discipline
in the Humanities
Classroom

Dissonant
Methods

UNIVERSITY *of* **ALBERTA** PRESS

Published by

University of Alberta Press
1-16 Rutherford Library South
11204 89 Avenue NW
Edmonton, Alberta, Canada T6G 2J4
uap.ualberta.ca

Copyright © 2020 Ada S. Jaarsma &
Kit Dobson

Library and Archives Canada
Cataloguing in Publication

Title: Dissonant methods : undoing discipline
  in the humanities classroom / Ada S. Jaarsma
  & Kit Dobson, editors.
Names: Jaarsma, Ada S., editor. | Dobson, Kit,
  1979- editor.
Description: Includes bibliographical references
  and index.
Identifiers: Canadiana (print) 20200215507 |
  Canadiana (ebook) 20200215523 |
  ISBN 9781772124897 (softcover) |
  ISBN 9781772125276 (PDF) |
  ISBN 9781772125252 (EPUB) |
  ISBN 9781772125269 (Kindle)
Subjects: LCSH: Humanities—Study and
  teaching (Higher) | LCSH: College
  teaching—Methodology. LCSH:
  Education, Higher—Aims and objectives.
Classification: LCC AZ182 .D57 2020 |
  DDC 001.3071/1—dc23

First edition, first printing, 2020.
First printed and bound in Canada by Houghton
Boston Printers, Saskatoon, Saskatchewan.
Copyediting and proofreading by
Kirsten Craven.
Indexing by Adrian Mather.

University of Alberta Press is committed to
protecting our natural environment. As part of
our efforts, this book is printed on Enviro Paper:
it contains 100% post-consumer recycled fibres
and is acid- and chlorine-free.

University of Alberta Press gratefully
acknowledges the support received for its
publishing program from the Government of
Canada, the Canada Council for the Arts, and
the Government of Alberta through the Alberta
Media Fund.

This book has been published with the help
of a grant from the Canadian Federation for
the Humanities and Social Sciences, through
the Awards to Scholarly Publications Program,
using funds provided by the Social Sciences and
Humanities Research Council of Canada.

Contents

I The Event

II Embodiment

III The Political

Acknowledgements

WE WOULD LIKE TO THANK Mount Royal University, the institution in which we both work, and our colleagues in the Department of Humanities and the Department of English, Languages, and Cultures. In addition, we acknowledge the support of Mount Royal University's Institute for the Scholarship of Teaching and Learning, and in particular the TransCanada Collaborative SoTL Grant that made this project possible. Finally, we would like to acknowledge the research assistants who helped with this project: Kyle Kinaschuk, Syd Peacock, Kaitlin Rothberger, and Amanda Lockhart. Thank you, finally, to the University of Alberta Press for supporting this project from its early stages.

Introduction

ADA S. JAARSMA

METHODS ANIMATE THE WORLD OF UNIVERSITY CLASSROOMS as
organizing logics that compel and constrain interactions among teachers and
students. This claim runs throughout the chapters of this collection. And it is
no neutral claim, of course. As Caroline Levine puts it, we run the promising
risk of becoming "canny formalists" when we pay close attention to the forms
that structure our institutional activities—and methods are one such form.[1]
The set-up of classroom spaces, the curricular commitments of programs, and
the hierarchies of universities: these are all examples of forms, according to
Levine. Other examples include the very rhythms by which we begin and wrap
up our classes, the pacing of our lessons, even the ways in which we hail our
students to participate in specific activities: these methods constitute some
of the forms by which teaching takes place.

Forms are abstract organizing principles, and they afford different
arrangements, relations, and activities; what forms have in common is that they
are iterable and portable. As Levine puts it, forms migrate across contexts.[2]
A bounded whole (like a classroom) will always exclude, Levine explains, and
a template (like a syllabus) will always repeat. It can be difficult to notice the
forms that we inhabit and deploy precisely because we inherit them from other
contexts. Why do we organize our classes as seminars, Levine asks?[3] Why do

we assume that this form, as opposed to the myriad of other possible scenarios, lends itself best to teaching and learning? These are the kinds of questions that preoccupy a canny formalist. If we can track the organizing movements of forms, across space and time and within our own classrooms, then we can become more attuned to their disruptive or emancipatory potential.[4]

In order to render the forms at play within our classrooms more recognizable, several contributors to this volume make use of a term that might, at first glance, strike the reader as absurdist. The term is "tomato," and it comes from a scene in Zadie Smith's novel, *On Beauty*, in which the methods employed by instructors are designated as specific kinds of *tomatoes*. Vee is an undergraduate whose fine-grained acuity about the differences between classrooms leads her to classify courses as tomatoes: "Professor Simeon's class is 'The tomato's nature versus the tomato's nurture,'" Vee explains, "and Jane Colman's class is 'To properly understand the tomato, you must first uncover the tomato's suppressed Herstory.'"[5] Each technique is so determining of the kind of teaching that takes place in a given classroom that Vee and her classmates refer to courses by their breed of tomato rather than calendar name: "Tomatoes 1670–1900," for example. On this basis, Vee informs her art history professor that, in his classroom, students must refrain from sharing their delight at Rembrandt paintings: "'Your class is all about never *ever* saying *I like the tomato*.'"[6]

Like any other form, tomatoes lay claim to particular affordances, and in this case, the affordances have to do with the nature of in-class discussion. As Vee explains, to participate successfully in this art history classroom, as a student, is to comment critically on artwork and avoid sentimental declarations like "I like that painting." In contrast, Vee describes her own father, a professor with archly religious views, in these terms: "Tomatoes Save."[7] It is likely that sentimental statements in that classroom will be welcomed, even drawn forth by the tomato's evangelical fervour. The term "tomato" foregrounds the specificity, even the singularity, of teaching methods: each tomato manifests its own flavour or recipe for what should take place in classrooms. (Part I of this book, "The Event," examines the stakes involved with recognizing the singularity of teaching methods.) The term "tomato" also calls our attention to the dissonance between classrooms: since undergraduate students move from classroom to classroom, they must adapt to the differing expectations and mandates of specific tomatoes.[8] (Part II, "Embodiment," lays out concrete practices that affirm, in varying ways, certain dissonant experiences within classrooms.) The term, in turn, prompts discussion about the overarching norms that should or should not govern the formal attributes of tomatoes. (Part III, "The Political," points to the exclusions that dissonant methods risk enacting or reinforcing.)

The chapters in this collection are fascinated, each in their own way, by the workings of tomatoes. No "tomato" or bundled set of pedagogical techniques emerges fully formed when instructors first begin teaching; rather, their pedagogical methods reflect, to varying degrees of fidelity, the instruction they themselves experienced as a student, likely in the context of a specific discipline.[9] And disciplines are devoted to forms. As Levine explains, there are forms at play within how we read, analyze, and even decide upon our objects of inquiry. Delineating a historical period, as a historian, involves the form of periodization.[10] Plotting a novel, as a creative writer, involves the form of narrative.[11] Disciplines as a whole might be described as relatively consistent reiterations of norms and practices.[12] Teaching, along these lines, is often a matter of reproducing and instilling these forms in students. Philosophy, for example, can be understood "as it is practiced, specifically as it appears in our classrooms."[13] Moreover, if we consider the forms at play within universities more broadly, then, as Mel Y. Chen claims, we notice that discipline "goes much further than disciplinarity."[14] Michel Foucault, for example, points to the time-table as a medieval form that now organizes modern panoptical institutions like the university.[15] The clock on the wall in our classrooms, in other words, is a formal element, one that solicits efficiency from instructors and students alike.

Along these lines, sometimes forms reinforce each other, as in the case of the consonance between the marketing tactics of finance capitalism and the practices of neoliberal universities. Students, tasked with navigating the university as consumers, often understand the teaching practices of their instructors to be oriented toward assessment, first and foremost. According to this logic, the classroom is a space to enter and inhabit because it will launch students into a world of competition for jobs, security, and entrepreneurial self-financing. (Tomatoes that reflect such logics will deploy methods designed to help students to become *homo oeconomicus*, persons who approach every-thing as a market and know only market conduct.[16] Such teaching practices might share the designation that Vee assigns to her father's methods—namely, "Tomatoes Save"—except that salvation in this instance hinges upon selling one's self and one's future in the marketplace.) It makes great sense, in such contexts, to relate to one's instructor as an assessor: as the person who is important insofar as they are assigning grades. The form that structures these interactions is an aggregate: the GPA.

Sometimes, however, forms collide in dissonant ways, and this dissonance is where Levine places her hope for the possibility of resistance and transform-ation.[17] This is also the vested interest of this collection, and the reason for its title, *Dissonant Methods*. Disciplines shape the methods that teachers create and deploy, but, as Chen suggests, disciplines are also partial; when we engage the promising partiality of our disciplines, "canonical vocabularies become gently imperiled within such imagined spaces."[18] In an essay titled "Tempo and Reading Well," Christa Davis Acampora points to the dissonance that students in New York City experience, rushing from work to family obligations to the university itself—where "once inside, the rhythm slows to an increasingly frustrating pace."[19] Rhythm is a form, on Levine's account, but the tempo of classrooms can change up by means of the artful deployment of teaching methods. Classroom rhythms might shift, Acampora explains, from plodding to energetic, engaged and interactive, and such changes will likely take place in "an instant."[20]

The extent to which instructors are free to draw forth such shifts is a question that this collection, as a whole, explores. Each chapter examines how the organizing power of neoliberal forms can be compromised, rerouted or deflected through the inventive methods of teaching.[21] Methods that are at odds with neoliberal imperatives, for example, operate according to other logics than assessment or panoptical surveillance. As Martin Shuster writes, in the first chapter's opening paragraph, teaching might prepare students to tap new desires and unknown possibilities, rather than preparing them solely for a world of labour and competition. Shuster examines the impact of neoliberal pressures upon the very meaning of education, making the case for classrooms as spaces that safeguard and solicit dissonance.

By foregrounding teaching, this book returns, in a way, to the early call of the Scholarship of Teaching and Learning (SoTL) for teachers to relate to teaching as a "scholarly" practice in its own right. Ernest Boyer's 1990 report, *Scholarship Reconsidered: Priorities of the Professoriate*, noted the devaluation of teaching, especially in relation to academic ambitions and achievements. "After all," he wrote, "it's futile to talk about improving the quality of teaching if, in the end, faculty are not given recognition for the time they spend with students."[22] Boyer made the case for an understanding of teaching *as scholarship*: subject to review, replete with expertise, deserving of inquiry.

This focus on teaching shifted, over subsequent decades, to one on learning. In an account of current SoTL practices, for example, Peter Felton identifies its first principle as "inquiry focused on student learning,"[23] and many definitions of SoTL begin with this representative question: "Are my students learning?"[24] This shift aligns with what might be described as the "learnification" of higher education, a broad-based turn toward neoliberal policies and practices.[25] This neologism, coined by Gert Biesta, sums up many of the concerns of this book's contributors: on his account, "learnification" refers to institutions in which students are "learners," teaching is about "creating learning opportunities," and universities are "places for learning."[26] Above all, "learnification" reflects the impact of neoliberal policies that place responsibility upon individuals.[27] In such contexts, as Biesta explains, there is dissonance when we invoke teachers as *persons* (rather than as factors that are more or less effective and efficient) and describe teaching as an event (in which students learn *something* from *someone*).[28] Such dissonance holds potential for emancipation or at least some critical distance from the imperatives of neoliberalism as they bear upon our classroom practices and relationships.

There is also dissonance within an enterprise like the Scholarship of Teaching and Learning when teaching retains (or regains) a certain primacy of emphasis. As Jonathan Kramnick and Anahid Nersessian argue, what counts as an explanation and what works as a "form" by which to forge explanatory models are disciplinary matters: disciplines are "epistemic domains operating under a set of local and shifting, yet still reliable, constraints."[29] Given that SoTL inquiry is undertaken by scholars operating within particular disciplinary contexts, it follows that such research will give rise to a wide range of explanations of the phenomena of "teaching" and "learning." This collection is invested in this kind of richly dissonant or pluralistic inquiry, given that, as Kramnick and Nersessian put it, "questions drive the work that we do, and explanatory terms follow in their wake."[30] That said, it is also committed to the very "promiscuous realism" that tends to characterize work in the humanities.[31] And so our subtitle, *Undoing Discipline in the Humanities Classroom*, speaks to this double meaning of "dissonance": the very plurality of methods by which to make sense of teaching (and learning) and the plurality of the humanities itself, especially the plurality of forms, perspectives, and even ontologies.

The book begins, along these lines, with chapters that foreground "the event" of teaching. As Kyle Kinaschuk explores in his chapter, we encounter indeterminacy even when it comes to delineating an event, like teaching, as such. (Rachel Jones echoes this point later on in the book, as well.) The event cannot be predicted, and it cannot be secured by repeating rote methods, as if the conditions for "learning" can be put into place and utilized time and again in the same way. Rather, the event that Biesta describes as "being taught by" is an encounter that likely undoes such conditions. Dissonance, in this context, is a radically existential term: it refers to a kind of rupture, on the part of the student, such that this student's very approach to knowledge is different, after the event. In her chapter, Kathy Cawsey situates the event in relation to a specific set of circumstances, the Dalhousie Dentistry scandal; this chapter raises questions about the interplay of reading literary narratives, texts from a distant historical and geographical world, in relation to contemporary narratives taking place on social media. Cawsey explores the ramifications of existential dissonance that each subsequent chapter, in its own way, elaborates: namely, the risk that the burden of attending to violence falls disproportionately on the most vulnerable bodies in our classrooms.

These reflections on the affective dimensions of classrooms, in turn, constitute the focus of Part II, organized around the theme of embodiment. In their chapters, Katja Pettinen and Guy Obrecht lay out concrete practices that instructors might deploy in order to draw out the embodied significance of classroom interactions. Dissonance, in this context, refers to several scenarios. In Pettinen's chapter, the very form of teaching practice itself takes dissonant shape. Rather than presuming that teachers are experts who instill knowledge in their students, we might teach in ways that respect individuals as "living systems existing within a multitude of co-evolutionary relations." As such a claim attests, teaching hails students as biosocial rather than disembodied learners, while also acknowledging the pragmatic import of knowledge acquisition itself. Turning to martial arts as an example, Pettinen elaborates an approach to teaching (and learning) in which embodied knowledge emerges in and through corporeal movements that take place over time.

Along similar lines, Obrecht tells the tale of his own search for dissonant methods of teaching, a tale in which "dissonance" takes on the musical resonances of appreciating dissonant tones, melody, and metre. As Obrecht puts it, "we hear with our bodies," a phrase that echoes closely the insights of preceding chapters. Each of these chapters invites us, as readers, into dissonant conversations in which scientific research is drawn together with philosophy, anthropology, or music theory; the impact of such dissonance extends to bodily habits and capacities, and it opens up dynamic possibilities for teachers beyond the role of authoritative expert.

Part III, "The Political," draws out the ramifications of dissonant methods in classrooms. Namrata Mitra explores the significance of curricular choices, especially in terms of how we ask our students to enact methods like the "close reading" of literary texts. As Mitra's own examples attest, students deploy their interpretative habits in ways that might be more or less dissonant with an instructor's own normative or political commitments. How should we teach postcolonial texts, for example, in classrooms in which students tend to uphold highly colonial presumptions? Mitra describes an in-class activity, devised for a classroom beset with precisely this predicament, and reflects on how it reorganizes the logics of students and their reading methods. Similarly, as Rachel Jones asks, how should we model and, in turn, ask our students to participate in anti-racist critique in classrooms where students experience the impact of racializing violence in highly disproportionate ways? Put otherwise, how should we redress the kinds of habits and actions that Beth Loffreda and Claudia Rankine describe as the "whiteness of whiteness"[32] and what Robin DiAngelo diagnoses as "white fragility,"[33] especially when such behaviour emerges in our own classrooms (often, as Loffreda, Rankine, and DiAngelo argue, as resentful responses by white students to anti-racist curriculum)? Jones explores these quandaries in depth, looking to an array of critical race scholars for insights into how to respect the differences of lived experiences while resolutely saying "no" to racializing violence. There is no outside of form, as Levine's account makes clear, but there is the methodological hope of "canny formalism." The three sections of this collection each seek to warrant this hope by identifying and reflecting upon the formal constraints and possibilities of teaching methods.

This collection as a whole seeks to contribute to conversations within SoTL and beyond about the import of the arts and humanities for insights into teaching.[34] Specifically, it offers a robust response to queries about the *theory* at play within SoTL inquiry.[35] This response involves attending to the form of teaching practices. As Levine puts it, "reading the rhythms of the world *in a formalist fashion*"[36] is a practice that lends itself to the interests and training of those of us who teach in the arts and humanities. We might also describe the methodological commitments of this book as an "experimental humanities," an approach to inquiry that is based explicitly in praxis—in this case, the praxis of teaching.[37] This project, in other words, offers a range of "praxiographic" reflections on the nature and import of teaching methods.[38]

As a whole, though, this collection seeks to disrupt any overly consonant message about teaching or teaching methods. (In Levine's terms, we want to alleviate the "ontological distress" of trying to resolve multiple forms into a unity).[39] We do this in several ways. First, several contributors confess to their own "tomatoes," flagging to the reader that their own perspectives likely differ from those of other pedagogues. Pettinen, for example, names and enacts this tomato: "A tomato is not a vegetable but a fruit (unless it is)." This tomato has two moves, moves that are slightly dissonant with each other: students encounter the legitimacy of scientific knowledge (in which the correct taxonomical understanding of tomatoes, for example, is that of "fruit" and not vegetable), but they also meet its pragmatic limitations (in which the cultural tendency is to eat tomatoes alongside vegetables, not other fruit, despite the classifications by scientists). Mitra's tomato, in contrast, enacts this tomato: "My Tomato is a Frame." This tomato locates the action in a different place, namely in the shifting form of "the frame" of analysis itself. As Mitra explains, the very frame that delimits one's understanding is what undergoes transformation in this tomato's classroom.

Second, two short pieces punctuate the rest of the collection, intermezzos that foreground more explicitly the role of students in classroom encounters. The first, written by Ely Shipley, draws us into an activity as if we, as readers, are Shipley's own students. Tasked with writing a poem, a task that might awaken anxiety or foreboding, we move through a set of prompts that Shipley, our poet-teacher, promises will afford us the capacity to produce our own poetic creations. The second is written by Kaitlin Rothberger, a student who participated in the three-day workshop in which the initial drafts of these chapters were first presented and discussed. Held at the Banff Centre on May 25 through 27, 2016, this workshop brought together graduate students, under-graduate students, and faculty members in order to experiment collaboratively with the forms of teaching practices. Rothberger's piece, perhaps more than any other chapter in this collection, reminds us that students often experience dissonance within classrooms—and that such dissonance is not always edifying or emancipatory. Rothberger's reflections caution us against any overly hasty enthusiasms about our own tomato-ambitions, while also raising the stakes for our own experiments in method.[40]

This project, funded by the Institute for the Scholarship of Teaching and Learning at Mount Royal University, took place over the course of several years: in the first year, participants read shared texts; in the second year, at the three-day workshop, we presented lesson plans and interacted with each other's methods and theoretical reflections on method; over the course of the third year, we completed these chapters, while in continued conversation with each other's drafts and research. While the hope of this project is grand in scope, holding out real possibilities for undermining neoliberal practices and the myriad forms of oppression that pervade classrooms and universities, it is also quite ordinary. We hope the pleasures and creative play of teaching, described by each contributor in their own way, prompt newfound joy on the part of our readers, whether you are students or teachers or administrators. And that the formal attributes of classrooms become newly open for dissonant encounters that stage the significance, if also the provisional nature, of teaching methods.

NOTES

1. Caroline Levine, *Forms: Whole, Rhythm, Hierarchy, Network* (Princeton: Princeton University Press, 2015), 150.
2. Levine, 7.
3. Levine, 47–48.
4. Levine, 45.
5. Zadie Smith, *On Beauty* (New York: Penguin, 2006), 312.
6. Smith, 312.
7. Smith, 313.
8. Ada S. Jaarsma, "Tomatoes in the Classroom," in *Kierkegaard after the Genome: Science, Existence and Belief in this World* (New York: Palgrave MacMillan, 2017), 155. See also Aislinn O'Donnell, "Experimentation in Institutions: Ethics, Creativity and Existential Competence," *Studies in Philosophy and Education* (2017), https://doi.org/10.1007/s11217-017-9572-5.
9. As scholars working in the Scholarship of Teaching and Learning might put it, teaching is a developmental activity. See Gary Poole and Nancy L. Chick, "On the Nature of Expertise in SoTL," *Teaching & Learning Inquiry* 4.2 (2016): 2.
10. Levine, *Forms*, 56.
11. Levine, 40.
12. Levine, 61.
13. Stephen Bloch-Schulman, "A Critique of Methods in the Scholarship of Teaching and Learning in Philosophy," *Teaching and Learning Inquiry* 4.1 (2016): 2. See also Sheila Lintott and Lissa Skitolsky, "Inclusive Pedagogy: Beyond Simple Content," *Hypatia* 31.2 (2016).
14. Mel Y. Chen, "Brain Fog: The Race for Cripistemology," *Journal of Literary and Cultural Disability Studies* 8.2 (2014): 178.
15. Michel Foucault, *Discipline and Punish: The Birth of the Prison*, trans. Alan Sheridan (London: Penguin, 1977), 137, 141, 156–57.
16. Wendy Brown, *Undoing the Demos: Neoliberalism's Stealth Revolution* (Cambridge, MA: Zone, 2015), 39.
17. Levine, *Forms*, 28.
18. Chen, "Brain Fog," 181. Within the context of the Scholarship of Teaching and Learning, for example, disciplinary methods often collide, making space for productive questions about the limits as well as import of specific epistemic approaches. See Karen Manarin, "Reading the Stories of Teaching and Learning," *Teaching & Learning Inquiry* 5.1 (2017): 7.

19. Christa Davis Acampora, "Tempo and Reading Well," in *Making Teaching and Learning Matter: Transformative Spaces in Higher Education*, ed. Judith Summerfield and Cheryl C. Smith (New York: Springer, 2011), 220.

20. Acampora, 226.

21. Levine, *Forms*, 132.

22. Ernest L. Boyer, *Scholarship Reconsidered: Priorities of the Professoriate* (Stanford: Carnegie Foundation, 1990), xi.

23. Peter Felton, "Principles of Good Practice in SoTL," *Teaching & Learning Inquiry* 1.1 (2013): 122.

24. Laurie K. Dickson and Melinda M. Treml, "Using Assessment and SoTL to Enhance Student Learning," *New Directions for Teaching & Learning* 136 (2013): 7.

25. Gert Biesta, *Good Education in an Age of Measurement* (Boulder, CO: Paradigm Publishers, 2010). See Carolin Kreber, "Furthering the 'Theory Debate' in the Scholarship of Teaching: A Proposal Based on MacIntyre's Account of Practices," *Canadian Journal of Higher Education* 45.2 (2015): 101.

26. Gert Biesta, "What Is Education For? On Good Education, Teacher Judgement, and Educational Professionalism," *European Journal of Education* 50.2 (2015): 76.

27. Rajani Naidoo, "Universities in the Marketplace: The Distortion of Teaching and Research," in *Reshaping the University: New Relationships between Research, Scholarship and Teaching*, ed. Ronald Barnett (New York: McGraw-Hill Education, 2003).

28. Gert Biesta, "Receiving the Gift of Teaching: From 'Learning From' to 'Being Taught By'," *Studies in Philosophy and Education* 32.5 (2013).

29. Jonathan Kramnick and Anahid Nersessian, "Form and Explanation," *Critical Inquiry* 43 (2017): 664.

30. Kramnick and Nersessian, 668.

31. Kramnick and Nersessian, 667. This is a citation from John Dupré's *The Disorder of Things: Metaphysical Foundations of the Disunity of Science* (Cambridge: Harvard University Press, 1993), 37–59.

32. Beth Loffreda and Claudia Rankine, introduction to *The Racial Imaginary: Writers on Race in the Life of the Mind*, ed. Claudia Rankine, Beth Loffreda, and Max King Cap (Albany, NY: Fence Books, 2015), 15.

33. Robin DiAngelo, "White Fragility," *The International Journal of Critical Pedagogy* 3.3 (2011).

34. See the special issue, "SoTL through the Lens of the Arts and Humanities," *The Canadian Journal for the Scholarship of Teaching and Learning* 6.2 (2015), http://ir.lib.uwo.ca/cjsotl_rcacea/vol6/iss2/.

35. Kreber, "Furthering the 'Theory Debate,'" 102.

36. Levine, *Forms*, 51; emphasis added.

37. Ed Finn, *What Algorithms Want: Imagination in the Age of Computing* (Cambridge, MA: MIT Press, 2017), 13.

38. Annemarie Mol, *The Body Multiple: Ontology in Medical Practice* (Durham, NC: Duke University Press, 2002), 33, 53, 83, 121.

39. Levine, *Forms*, 42. Moreover, this collection seeks to open up the very nature of "method" itself. As Levine explains, "To isolate a single form and assume its dominance is almost always an act of oversimplification" (100).

40. Rothberger, among other contributors to the book, participates in ongoing conversations that emerged out of this project in the form of a series of audio essays. To hear these discussions, go to http://thelearninggene.com/episodes/.

WORKS CITED

Acampora, Christa Davis. "Tempo and Reading Well." In *Making Teaching and Learning Matter: Transformative Spaces in Higher Education*, edited by Judith Summerfield and Cheryl C. Smith, 219–36. New York: Springer, 2011.

Biesta, Gert. *Good Education in an Age of Measurement*. Boulder, CO: Paradigm Publishers, 2010.

———. "Receiving the Gift of Teaching: From 'Learning From' to 'Being Taught By'." *Studies in Philosophy and Education* 32.5 (2013): 449–61.

———. "What Is Education For? On Good Education, Teacher Judgement, and Educational Professionalism." *European Journal of Education* 50.2 (2015): 75–87.

Bloch-Schulman, Stephen. "A Critique of Methods in the Scholarship of Teaching and Learning in Philosophy." *Teaching & Learning Inquiry* 4.1 (2016). http://dx.doi.org/10.20343/teachlearninqu.4.1.10.

Boyer, Ernest L. *Scholarship Reconsidered: Priorities of the Professoriate*. Stanford: Carnegie Foundation, 1990.

Brown, Wendy. *Undoing the Demos: Neoliberalism's Stealth Revolution*. Cambridge, MA: Zone, 2015.

Chen, Mel Y. "Brain Fog: The Race for Cripistemology." *Journal of Literary and Cultural Disability Studies* 8.2 (2014): 171–84.

DiAngelo, Robin. "White Fragility." *The International Journal of Critical Pedagogy* 3.3 (2011): 54–70.

Dickson, Laurie K., and Melinda M. Treml. "Using Assessment and SoTL to Enhance Student Learning." *New Directions for Teaching & Learning* 136 (2013): 7–16.

Dupré, John. *The Disorder of Things: Metaphysical Foundations of the Disunity of Science*. Cambridge: Harvard University Press, 1993.

Felton, Peter. "Principles of Good Practice in SoTL." *Teaching & Learning Inquiry* 1.1 (2013): 121–25.

Finn, Ed. *What Algorithms Want: Imagination in the Age of Computing*. Cambridge, MA: MIT Press, 2017.

Foucault, Michel. *Discipline and Punish: The Birth of the Prison*. Translated by Alan Sheridan. London: Penguin, 1977.

Jaarsma, Ada S. "Tomatoes in the Classroom." In *Kierkegaard after the Genome: Science, Existence and Belief in this World*, 139–70. New York: Palgrave Macmillan, 2017.

Kramnick, Jonathan, and Anahid Nersessian. "Form and Explanation." *Critical Inquiry* 43 (2017): 650–69.

Kreber, Carolin. "Furthering the 'Theory Debate' in the Scholarship of Teaching: A Proposal Based on MacIntyre's Account of Practices." *Canadian Journal of Higher Education* 45.2 (2015): 99–115.

Levine, Caroline. *Forms: Whole, Rhythm, Hierarchy, Network*. Princeton: Princeton University Press, 2015.

Lintott, Sheila, and Lissa Skitolsky. "Inclusive Pedagogy: Beyond Simple Content." *Hypatia* 31.2 (2016): 447–59.

Loffreda, Beth, and Claudia Rankine. Introduction to *The Racial Imaginary: Writers on Race in the Life of the Mind*. Edited by Claudia Rankine, Beth Loffreda, and Max King Cap, 13–22. Albany, NY: Fence Books, 2015.

Manarin, Karen. "Reading the Stories of Teaching and Learning." *Teaching & Learning Inquiry* 5.1 (2017). http://dx.doi.org/10.20343/5.1.13.

Mol, Annemarie. *The Body Multiple: Ontology in Medical Practice*. Durham, NC: Duke University Press, 2002.

Naidoo, Rajani. "Universities in the Marketplace: The Distortion of Teaching and Research." In *Reshaping the University: New Relationships between Research, Scholarship and Teaching*, edited by Ronald Barnett, 27–36. New York: McGraw-Hill Education, 2003.

O'Donnell, Aislinn. "Experimentation in Institutions: Ethics, Creativity and Existential Competence." *Studies in Philosophy and Education* (2017). https://doi.org/10.1007/s11217-017-9572-5.

Poole, Gary, and Nancy L. Chick. "On the Nature of Expertise in SoTL." *Teaching & Learning Inquiry* 4.2 (2016). http://dx.doi.org/10.20343/10.20343/teachlearninqu.4.2.1.

Smith, Zadie. *On Beauty*. New York: Penguin, 2006.

"SoTL through the Lens of the Arts and Humanities." Special issue. *The Canadian Journal for the Scholarship of Teaching and Learning* 6.2 (2015). http://ir.lib.uwo.ca/cjsotl_rcacea/vol6/iss2/.

I

The Event

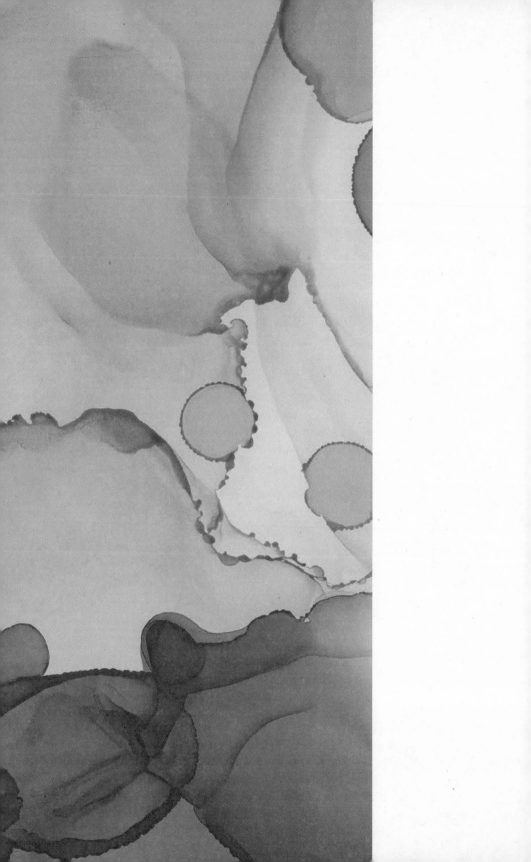

Education for the World

MARTIN SHUSTER

THERE IS CURRENTLY A GROWING, and, to my mind, deeply mistaken understanding of education as somehow concerned with preparing students "for the world," where that is understood narrowly as preparation for a job. Is *that* the world for which we are preparing students? Merely the world of labour and jobs, of workdays and years? Is this how we measure a world? On one hand, of course, it just is a fact that this *is* our world: ours *is* a world of jobs and of money. On the other hand, our world, at least presently, admits of more—of things yet to come and possibilities yet unknown, not to mention desires thought lost and currents lain dormant and hidden. My aims in what follows are to sketch a more robust understanding of "world" and its relationship to education, one that allows us to see both the importance of preparing students for the world, and the necessity of expanding any such understanding of "world" to include far more than preparation for the labour force.

In an essay on Oswald Spengler and Ludwig Wittgenstein, titled "Declining Decline: Wittgenstein as a Philosopher of Culture," Stanley Cavell suggests that Wittgenstein's "*Investigations* can be seen as a philosophy of culture, one that relates itself to its time as a time in which the continuation of philosophy is at stake."[1] Compare this remark to Theodor W. Adorno's remark that "philosophy, which once appeared obsolete, sustains itself because the moment for its actualization has been lost."[2] The former idea seems to be that Wittgenstein's entire *Philosophical Investigations* is somehow presented as a way to continue philosophy, to make its continuation (in the present moment) possible; the implied suggestion is that without this, philosophy would come to an end. Adorno's suggestion, on the other hand, seems to be that philosophy continues *because* it has not been actualized; we somehow failed to do something important that would *make* it obsolete. Note that both Cavell and Adorno appear to think that philosophy *can* come to an end. And yet—what are these two conceptions of philosophy? And what—if anything—do they have to recommend to our present moment?[3]

Philosophy of/as/and Dissonance

And, equally importantly, why gift such importance to philosophy, especially in the present moment? Why *either* fear or desire its end? In part, it seems that we have no choice—one might say the "market" has decided: philosophy is seen as an unjustifiable extravagance, an absurdity that destroys one's prospects in the world; that ruins one's career possibilities.[4] At the same time, philosophy's power is broadly understood, caged but kept alive for years like a ransomed prisoner; it's known—consciously or unconsciously—that philosophy is key both to unlocking our inheritance and to investing that inheritance into something new. Whether you speak of democracy or forgiveness, of human reason and distinction, or of human wickedness and folly, you speak of and for and with philosophy. To the extent that our problems are human problems—tied to what we say and do and think—then our problems are philosophical problems, tied to the histories, genealogies, and assessments of what we say and do and think. Our solutions too, then, are—indeed, must be—philosophical. In this context, note the similarities in the following two images, the first proposed by Wittgenstein, the second by Adorno:[5]

> Philosophical problems can be compared to locks on safes, which can be opened by dialing a certain word or number, so that no force can open the door until just this word has been hit upon, and once it is hit upon any child can open it.[6]

> As a constellation, theoretical thought circles the concept it would like to unseal, hoping that it may fly open like the lock of a well-guarded safe-deposit box: in response, not to a single key or a single number, but to a combination of numbers.[7]

In both cases, the "solution" to a philosophical problem is something that one hits upon precisely and decisively: there just is a way to *solve* a philosophical problem; philosophical problems are not perennial (and, indeed, perhaps thinking that they are is itself a distinct sort of philosophical problem, one that itself is also not perennial). Let me flesh out these two contexts so that I might say more about what unites and differentiates them.

There are two things animating Adorno's thought. The first is the Marxist thought, found in Marx's eleventh thesis on Feuerbach, that "philosophers have only *interpreted* the world, in various ways; the point, however, is to *change* it."[8] The second idea, likely found in differing ways, both in Benjamin and Hegel, is the idea that a utopian world is a world without contradiction, a world in which no dialectical thought can gain purchase, because the contradictions that would drive the dialectical motor simply do not exist. In such a world, there is no need for philosophy.[9] Obviously, we do not live in such a world. To someone like Adorno or to others—say, for someone in 1776 with the Declaration of Independence in the United States, or in 1789 at the cusp of the French Revolution, or 1791 in Haiti, or in 1873 at the end of the American Civil War, or for students in 1968, or for an exhausted world in 2008 with the election of an unlikely senator named Barack Obama to the presidency of the United States—perhaps it *looked like* we might live in such a world, but we know now—as Adorno seemed to realize—that we do not. What then is the role of the philosopher and of philosophy? Adorno's thought seems to be that philosophy sustains itself because it is the mode through which we aim to address the contradictions that still exist in our world. In this way, there is room both for a descriptive function (to figure out *what* and *how* those contradictions work) and a prescriptive one (to recommend what ought to be done, practically, in order to remove those contradictions and the suffering caused by their effects).[10] Historically and famously, there is an important point to note about Adorno in this respect: he clearly thought, following Marx, that there was a time for description and a time for prescription, and that the two times need not always—if ever—overlap. Indeed, there may be a wrong time for one or the other, and it is important to assess and understand when the proper time for each is. This, then, is a third function for philosophy in Adorno's eyes. As Marx puts it, "What is to be done, and done immediately, at any given, particular moment in the future, depends, of course, wholly and entirely on the actual historical circumstances in which action is to be taken."[11] Philosophy then comes to an end when the *need* for it comes to an end; in other words, when there is nothing to drive the dialectical motor, when human social arrangements (and thereby human existence) are free of dissonance, taken here as an analogue for suffering.[12] When Obama's foreign policy turns out to accelerate George W. Bush's pursuits of misery, and when Donald J. Trump's politics of change through fear follow Obama's politics of change through hope, then the need for philosophy lives on.

Nothing in Cavell's conception of philosophy undermines this Marx-Adorno picture, but Cavell does—following Wittgenstein—inflect it in a distinct way, bringing a dimension of it to light that Marx and Adorno largely neglect. Cavell frequently quotes the following passages by Wittgenstein and Emerson. The first, found in Wittgenstein, reads that "what *we* do [with Wittgenstein's brand of philosophy] is to bring words back from their metaphysical to their everyday use."[13] The second, found in Emerson, reads as follows: "Conformity makes them [most people] not false in a few particulars, authors of a few lies, but false in all particulars. Their every truth is not quite true. Their two is not the real two, their four not the real four; so that every word they say chagrins us and we know not where to begin to set them right."[14] One way to understand how Cavell is combining and modulating these two passages is to see him acknowledging the exact stance that orients Adorno's thinking: that, as moderns—struggling in the wake of an accelerating capitalism, a decelerating presence of authority, and a disenchanting form of human thinking—we are characterized by a

> pervasive, irreducible recurrence of human nervousness or restlessness, as it were the human incapacity for and refusal of peace (which Wittgenstein specifically pictures as features of the modern subject, ones he portrays as torment, perverseness, disappointment, devastation, suffocation, and so on), a kind of perpetual preparation for violence that has led me to speak of our dealing among ourselves "the little deaths of everyday life," the slights, the grudges, the clumsiness, the impatience, the bitterness, the narcissism, the boredom, and so on (variously fed and magnified and inflamed by standing sources of social enmity, say, racism, sexism, elitism, and so on).[15]

Putting things in this way, it might seem as if I am pushing too far the analogy between Adorno on one hand, and Wittgenstein and Cavell, on the other. The latter might strike many as concerned with something different than Adorno, that is with a sort of suffering that is not *merely* social, but, say, constitutive of our existence as human *creatures*. Yet this argument fails to register the depth of Cavell's engagement with this issue, for he is clear in rejecting any idea of our culture—in other words, our society—"as [merely] a system of modification of our [somehow more basic] lives as talkers."[16] The ills mentioned above are "features of the modern subject." Follow Cavell, then, and understand that Wittgenstein's focus on skepticism about other minds and on the pain of others ought to be inflected through Emerson's focus on seeing significant cases and sites of pain as bound up with social failure, with the myriad ways in which society causes suffering and conformity to and with that suffering.[17] For Wittgenstein, neither pain nor suffering are a focus accidentally, as if *any* emotional or somatic component could have done the analytical work, for it is pain that explicitly broaches most fundamentally the fact that "there is a moral demand to respond to its expression."[18] What is the inflection that Cavell adds to this common thread about suffering that he shares with Adorno? Call it a *linguistic* inflection, one that stresses that what is at stake is an entire form of life (alternatively: an entire culture—that it is, in Emerson's words, "*every word they say chagrins us*" and for *this* reason "we know not where to begin to set them right," as if the task is too great, for the form of life, and everything that it implies and involves, is too vast to begin to interrogate in this way).[19] Anything we might conclude or learn about suffering, and thereby about others, depends on *what* we say, and how we say it, and, of course, to whom. Prioritize thereby Austin's claim in "A Plea for Excuses":

> When we examine what we should say when, what words we should use in what situations, we are looking again not *merely* at words (or "meanings," whatever they may be) *but also at the realities we use the words to talk about*: we are using a sharpened awareness of words to sharpen our perception of, though not as the final arbiter of, *the phenomena*.[20]

This is the tenor in which Wittgenstein's reflections on language ought to be taken; even the opening of Wittgenstein's *Investigations*—with its most basic scene of instruction, of *education*—is meant to correct any view of ourselves that suggests there is some way *outside* of seeing ourselves as intimately involved with the very construction, and thereby limits and parameters, of our world: thus the wrongness of Augustine's picture, where a child is some passive receptacle for words, as opposed to a distinct individual in an entire form of life, with everything that Cavell calls the "whirl of organism" that makes up what people *do* in addition to what they think (what they find humorous, and not; dangerous, and not; painful, and not—what they conceive of each of these as being, and how they delineate and understand the limits of the same and why, and so on).[21]

Cavell, Wittgenstein, and Adorno are thereby all philosophers of culture; and philosophy is ultimately at stake for all three not because philosophy is about to be completed, as if the world is entering some utopian phase, but rather because philosophy is in danger of disappearing, because the world is entering a phase wherein our *capacities for* philosophy are becoming deformed because the world itself is becoming (more) deformed, so that our capacities are themselves becoming a danger, turned against us, requisitioned for purposes that further undermine them, and thereby our world and its possibilities. Note, then, the importance—already present in the opening of the *Investigations*—of education, to and for the world: we are each daily, consistently, without pause or mercy, initiated into a form of life, our sensibilities formed by everything said and unsaid to us.

Cavell's claim (and again one to which Adorno is sympathetic) is that the possibility of dissonance—the motor that drives the dialectic—is itself under threat of dissolution, but not because the *need* for it will disappear, but because our ignorance of the need—indeed, needs—will multiply. For Adorno, the culture industry is this danger,[22] but so is our persistent ability and desire to repudiate our language, to sublime it, to locate ourselves as somehow outside of our language, ultimately to think that we can remove ourselves from it (in the quest for a false objectivity), as much as to resign ourselves to the ways in which we remove others from language (in the presence of a callousness or antipathy or animus as *the* mode of our acknowledgment).[23] To the extent that our philosophy registers dissonance, forces the acknowledgment of suffering and contradiction, then philosophy lives, and does so for a (good) reason. When philosophy fails meaningfully to register that dissonance, to acknowledge suffering, then it runs the risk of disappearing, as surely as if that dissonance did not exist in the first place (as in a utopia). As opposed to a utopia, the danger here is becoming the sort of "last humans" that Nietzsche describes, where there the only friction, where the only contact between us is the fact that we merely rub against each other for warmth.[24]

What is the significance of this story for education?

Dissonance and the World, Philosophy and the World

To return again to the Cavell essay referenced in my opening paragraph, Cavell notes that, "philosophy's virtue is responsiveness. What makes it philosophy is not that its response will be total, but that it will be tireless, awake when the others have all fallen asleep."[25] Cavell also notes that "philosophy lies in the practice, the commitment to go on in a certain way, call this discontinuously...in a particular refusal of endlessness, in an unguardedness, and openness."[26] Apart from their relevance for the (philosophy) classroom—where essentials include critique and openness, sincerity and seriousness, and a continuous assertion and revelation of one's subjectivity, an understanding of where one stands and why and how and what for—I take the significance of these thoughts to be even more radical. The procedures and possibilities of and for philosophy, and thereby of the (philosophy) classroom, are themselves of a kind with a particular way of having and inhabiting a world. In this context, let me raise a point that Audre Lorde stresses in her classic essay, "The Transformation of Silence into Language and Action." She opens by noting that "I have come to believe over and over again that what is most important to me *must be spoken, made verbal and shared*, even at the risk of having it bruised and misunderstood."[27] Lorde elaborates, noting, "to survive in the mouth of this dragon we call america, we have had to learn this first and most vital lesson—that we were never meant to survive. Not as human beings. And neither were most of you here today, Black or not...because the machine will try to grind you into dust anyway, whether or not we speak."[28] Take Lorde here implicitly to be referencing a Marxist-inspired tradition—one stressed by Adorno and others, and acknowledged certainly by Cavell—that highlights the extent to which, in late capitalism (now instantiated across the globe), individuals are "appendages of the machine."[29] Appendages are largely irrelevant; they are mere instantiations of a broader whole. On such a view, commodification, alienation, and exploitation[30] leads to a capitalist machinery within which individuals—whether they are CEOs or teachers, students or beggars, politicians or sanitation engineers—are plugged into roles, roles in which they are increasingly unable to feel "at home," and roles which are largely determined for them by means of the processes animating the appendage; the operations of this machinery are so total that human subjectivity (as much as human objectivity) is in danger of disappearing.[31]

The classroom is *not* unique in this regard: students and educators are beholden to an array of forces originating from broader market trends; acknowledging this fact is important to developing any sort of pedagogical response.[32] Furthermore, any such acknowledgment allows us to dismiss the idea that there is some sort of internal or unique crisis in or for the humanities; the crisis is external, and it is largely "a financial dispute fueled by panic."[33] Better yet: it's a financial crisis exacerbated by the form of monopolistic, exploitative, and brutal capitalism that's presently actualized. If that's the case, then the crisis of the humanities is best addressed by addressing the general crisis itself, by working to alter the economic—and thereby social and political—conditions that such a form of capitalism bequeaths to us.[34] This is not to say, however, that there is no crisis for humanities *education,* for it just is the case that our subjectivities—teacher and student alike—are formed in the world of late capitalism, and that thereby the structures of late capitalism have "settled into the character of people to their innermost center."[35] What such a state of affairs calls for is what Adorno terms "critical self-reflection," or "the power of reflection, of self-determination, of not cooperating."[36] Yet, if the effects of late capitalism are so pernicious and so wide-ranging with regard to human subjectivity, then this seems exactly the sort of reflection that is barred to subjects (thus, the emergence of one of the great worries of and for and in Adorno's thought).

Here, consider a thought of Hannah Arendt's. In her essay, "The Crisis in Education," Arendt notes that "the problem of education in the modern world lies in the fact that by its very nature it cannot forgo either authority or tradition, and yet must proceed in a world that is neither structured by authority nor held together by tradition."[37] In this context, it just is the case that late capitalism brokers no allegiance to anything except profit, and profit has use of authority or tradition only to the extent that it serves to propound its ends. In this vein, see this insight about capitalism as analogous to the way in which language more broadly functions: we speak in a language that is fundamentally not of our making (it is perpetually inherited); we speak in the condition of possibly being avoided, unacknowledged, or invisible, a state where our words might be misunderstood, ignored, or unheard. In short, we are appendages of language. Cavell puts both thoughts incredibly well when he stresses that "our relation to our language—to the fact that we are subject to expression and comprehension, victims of meaning—is accordingly a key to our sense of our distance from our lives, of our sense of the alien, of ourselves as alien to ourselves, thus alienated."[38] Modulate this thought with Cavell's suggestion that every claim we make is a claim we stake: a search for community, with the perpetual possibility that such community may not exist, the possibility that we just are alone.[39] Nonetheless, we speak, we are daily expressive, whether we aim to be or not—even our silence is itself expressive, if even only of despair—for the singular alternative to all of this "is having nothing to say, being voiceless,"[40] that is, not even being a *someone* for whom language *can* operate. Here is how Cavell proposes the thought:

> The interesting question for us cannot any longer be whether a
> serious impulse or idea will be debased or imitated or skinned for
> show. Of course the Beethoven Ninth will be used to throw out the
> news. Nor is it only the leopard which now becomes part of the

ceremony, but the stray cat. The interesting question, in a world
beset by seriousness—by fraudulent claims to its possession, and by
nauseated mockings of those claims, and by hearty or worldly efforts
to deny its existence—is whether room continues to be made for the
genuine article, and whether we will know it when we see it.[41]

The dangers of late capitalism, thereby, are of a kind, at least formally, with
the dangers inherent to language. Of course, the former are of a different
(and some would thereby argue more dangerous) sort: they might literally kill
you; but prioritizing these (material) dangers strikes me as both a weakness
of imagination and a misjudgment of what counts and must count here:
the levelling and polishing off of individuality, of completing ourselves into
Nietzsche's last humans—it all boils down to, as Adorno might put it, the
confirmation of "the philosopheme of pure identity as death." In other words,
the sufferings of the world of late capitalism are no longer exclusively those of
the fist or the iron or the whip, but equally those of emptiness and coldness
and despair...found equally and easily in any aspect of our being together,
whether in public, at our jobs, or in our homes.

In the classroom, in pedagogy, I take it that all of our commitments,
desires, and performances must be oriented toward one goal: expanding our
world. To do so, we hold the line against the forces that would diminish it,
even as we draw new lines of salience, new means of action, and new ways of
thinking (with the caveat that all of this stress on novelty should not imply
that such newness is not to be found by mining the past: think of Adorno's
image of a "combination of numbers," implying the possibility of old—even
forgotten or lost—things in new configurations).[42] World here is meant in the
deep phenomenological sense, as the idea, found prominently in phenomenol-
ogists like Husserl, Merleau-Ponty, and Heidegger, that we are first involved in
the world practically, in what might be termed "absorbed coping,"[43] where the
world presents to us lines of salience and action, possibilities for engagement,
occasions for thought, consequences for existence, and sites for experimentation and play (and this for better or for worse: it just is the case that these exist,
albeit in *qualitatively* depleted or "cold" ways; late capitalism is, too, a world,
albeit a significantly impoverished one).[44] In the classroom, one must reveal
one's standing within the form of life that is late capitalism even as one asks
students to do the same, all in relationship to texts and theories that provide
access to the foundations, conclusions, and insides of late capitalism.

To elaborate the world, to bring it qualitatively to life in this way, means
to acknowledge its ills, its limits, its deformations, and thereby to acknowledge

ourselves as in it, its ills as our ills, its limits as our limits, and its deformations as our deformations. In such an acknowledgment, note two distinct understandings of a *limit* (what the German Idealists distinguished as "Schranke" in contrast to "Grenze"): one understanding of limit is to see it as a border, similar to a border between countries, where one might look, or indeed even step, beyond it; another understanding of limit is to see it as a sort of ceiling, a boundary beyond which one will never go. It is important to see that late capitalism is the former, even though it often—indeed perhaps almost always— appears as the latter. Arendt notes that "education is the point at which we decide whether we love the world enough to assume responsibility for it."[45] Such an assumption requires our lodging and staking our claims *within* the world; in doing so, we thereby reveal an element of that world, provisionally even the simple fact that the world is such that we might imagine a different one; as Arendt notes, the world is constitutively of the form of an "in-between" (us). Training our students to pursue speech in such a manner, across a range of modalities and topics, is both to initiate them into a form of life, and thereby into a world ("when we examine what we should say when, what words we should use in what situations, we are looking again not merely at words... but also at the realities we use the words to talk about").[46] Such an approach embraces dissonance, for dissonance lights up the possibilities and impossibilities that animate each of us, that draw the limits of our world. To do this is as much to understand the world, and do so critically, unforgivingly, genealogically, historically, and yet still contingently prone to suffering, as it is to understand ourselves as contingently in it, thinking thereby of where and how we (might) stand in such a world, of what it might offer us, if anything. In education, this means being wed to great traditions even as we are willing—indeed, required— to expand the definitions of "great" and "tradition" irrevocably, beyond the parameters of space or time or media, finding ourselves fulfilled only in the process of using those traditions in current and thereby novel contexts, potentially usurping them and recasting them, proving that they have vibrancy, and that they *are* a world, and we in it...or as Cavell puts it, "the only return on becoming adult, the only justice in forgoing that world of possibility, is the reception of actuality—the pain and balm in the truth of the world: that it exists, and I in it."[47]

NOTES

1. Stanley Cavell, *This New Yet Unapproachable America: Lectures after Emerson after Wittgenstein* (Albuquerque, NM: Living Batch Press, 1989), 72.

2. Theodor W. Adorno, *Negative Dialectics*, trans. E.B. Ashton (New York: Continuum, 1973), 16.

3. I take it as a given that Wittgenstein's text, published in the 1950s but likely composed in the decade before, is contemporaneous with Adorno's own, published in the 1960s but also likely written prior; importantly, both texts are *contemporary* to our own moment, animated still by the problems that animated their moment. In this way, both thinkers are our contemporaries.

4. Most recently and prominently, see Senator Marco Rubio's comments in the United States Republican primary, that "we need more welders and less philosophers," because the former "make more money" than the latter (November 10, 2015, in Milwaukee). Although statistically the statement is false, the *perception* that Rubio presents and embodies is one upon which facts have no purchase, and this is something that also needs accounting for. Note that Rubio has since changed his opinion about philosophy; see Paul Fain, "Rubio Changes Tune on Philosophers," *Chronicle of Higher Education*, March 29, 2018, https://www.insidehighered.com/quicktakes/2018/03/29/rubio-changes-tune-philosophers.

5. Roger Foster originally drew my attention to these passages and their connections. In response to these connections, the thoughts that follow are my own.

6. Ludwig Wittgenstein, *Philosophical Occasions, 1912–1951*, ed. James C. Klagge and Alfred Nordmann (Indianapolis: Hackett, 1993), 176.

7. Adorno, *Negative Dialectics*, 163. See *Lectures on Negative Dialectics*, ed. Rolf Tiedemann, trans. Rodney Livingstone (Cambridge: Polity Press, 2008), 139.

8. Karl Marx, *The Marx-Engels Reader*, ed. Robert C. Tucker, 2nd ed. (New York: Norton, 1978), 145.

9. Incidentally, this is a thought that Richard Rorty shares, as when he invokes the idea of utopia as a "world of love." On this point, see Martin Shuster, "Rorty and (the Politics of) Love," *Graduate Faculty Philosophy Journal* 40.1 (2019).

10. In this way, for Adorno, "suffering" is the motor that guides this process. On this point, see my *Autonomy after Auschwitz: Adorno, German Idealism, and Modernity* (Chicago: University of Chicago Press, 2014), 71–134; as well as "Nothing to Know: The Epistemology of Moral Perfectionism in Adorno and Cavell," *Idealistic Studies* 44.1 (2015).

11. Marx to Nieuwenhuis (February 2, 1881), quoted in Theodor W. Adorno, *Gesammelte Schriften*, 20 vols. (Frankfurt am Main: Suhrkamp Verlag, 1984), 10:1:291; Fabian Freyenhagen, "Adorno's Politics Theory and Praxis in Germany's 1960s," *Philosophy & Social Criticism* 40.9 (2014): 868.

12. There is a lot more to be said here, for example, about suffering and its relationship to contradiction (see footnote eight above), and also about how *what* such a society would look like in its entirety is necessarily prohibited to us. See Martin Shuster, "Adorno and Negative Theology," *Graduate Faculty Philosophy Journal* 37.1 (2015).

13. Ludwig Wittgenstein, *Philosophical Investigations*, trans. G.E.M. Anscombe (Upper Saddle River, NJ: Prentice Hall, 1958), §116.

14. See "Self-Reliance" in Ralph Waldo Emerson, *The Essential Writings of Ralph Waldo Emerson* (New York: Modern Library, 2009). Quoted in Cavell, *This New Yet Unapproachable America*, 69.

15. Veena Das, *Life and Words: Violence and the Descent into the Ordinary* (Berkeley: University of California Press, 2007), xiii. There is a lot more that might be said about our status as "moderns." Some texts that I've found useful in this context are Hannah Arendt, "What Is Authority?" *Between Past and Future* (London: Penguin, 1968); Marshall Berman, *All That Is Solid Melts into Air: The Experience of Modernity* (New York: Simon and Schuster, 1983); Robert B. Pippin, *Modernism as a Philosophical Problem: On the Dissatisfaction of European High Culture*, 2nd ed. (Oxford: Blackwell, 1999); Charles Taylor, *Sources of the Self: The Making of the Modern Identity* (Cambridge, MA: Harvard University Press, 1989); *A Secular Age* (Cambridge, MA: Harvard University Press, 2007); Max Weber, "Science as Vocation," in *From Max Weber: Essays in Sociology*, ed. and trans. H.H. Gerth and C. Wright Mills (London: Routledge, 1948); "Politics as Vocation," in *From Max Weber: Essays in Sociology*, ed. and trans. H.H. Gerth and C. Wright Mills (London: Routledge, 1948); *The Protestant Ethic and the Spirit of Capitalism: And Other Writings*, trans. Peter Baehr and Gordon C. Wells (New York: Penguin, 2002).

16. Cavell, *This New Yet Unapproachable America*, 48.

17. On this point, see notably "Fate" in Emerson. See Cavell's remarks on this essay in Stanley Cavell, "Emerson's Constitutional Amending," in *Emerson's Transcendental Etudes*, ed. David Justin Hodge (Palo Alto: Stanford University Press, 2003).

18. Das, *Life and Words*, xi. Cf. Shuster, "Nothing to Know."

19. This thought is not so distinct from Adorno, but what is distinct are the parameters by which this happens. For Adorno, it is notably the process of the dialectic of enlightenment, while for Cavell it is something that has always been true but is exacerbated *in* modernity. On this point, see especially the end of my "Language and Loneliness: Arendt, Cavell, and Modernity," *International Journal of Philosophical Studies* 20.4 (2012). I have also tried to show that Adorno and Cavell are quite close on this point; see the first chapter of *Autonomy after Auschwitz*.

20. J.L. Austin, "A Plea for Excuses," in *Philosophical Papers* (Oxford: Oxford University Press, 1979), 182.

21. Stanley Cavell, "The Availability of Wittgenstein's Later Philosophy," in *Must We Mean What We Say?* (Cambridge, MA: Harvard University Press, 2002), 52.

22. See Deborah Cook, *The Culture Industry Revisited: Theodor W. Adorno on Mass Culture* (Lanham, MD: Rowman & Littlefield, 1996).

23. On this process, see the remarks in Martin Shuster, "On the Ethical Basis of Language: Some Themes in Davidson, Cavell, and Levinas," *Journal for Cultural and Religious Theory* 14.2 (2015).

24. Friedrich W. Nietzsche, *Thus Spoke Zarathustra*, trans. Adrian Del Caro (Cambridge: Cambridge University Press, 2006), 10, Prologue, §5.

25. Cavell, *This New Yet Unapproachable America*, 74.

26. Cavell, 73–74.

27. Audre Lorde, *Sister Outsider: Essays and Speeches* (New York: Crossing Press, 2012), 40; emphasis added.

28. Lorde, 42.

29. See Theodor W. Adorno, "Late Capitalism or Industrial Society?" in *Can One Live after Auschwitz? A Philosophical Reader*, ed. Rolf Tiedemann, trans. Rodney Livingstone (Palo Alto: Stanford University Press, 2003), 117. For an elaboration, see especially the first two chapters of Fabian Freyenhagen, *Adorno's Practical Philosophy: Living Less Wrongly* (Cambridge: Cambridge University Press, 2013).

30. Again, these are the three Marxist organizing diagnoses that are highlighted in the first chapter of Freyenhagen's *Adorno's Practical Philosophy*.

31. For more on this process, see the first chapter of Shuster, *Autonomy after Auschwitz*. Cf. Stanley Cavell, *The Claim of Reason: Wittgenstein, Skepticism, Morality, and Tragedy* (Oxford: Oxford University Press, 1979), 468. In the book, I sketch the contour of a problem that I have largely bracketed here, a problem about the possible authority of normativity, of *any* normative claim. I still think this is a problem, but it is one that is not central to the discussion here, which I think operates in a different register, one that occurs, say, after that problem might be resolved conceptually (as I allege in the book), or not (if you are not convinced by my solution). There are, of course, connections to be wrought here, but to bring them out would take me too far afield.

32. On this point, see especially the comments by Ada Jaarsma on the Scholarship of Teaching and Learning movement (SoTL) in Ada S. Jaarsma, "On Being Taught," *Canadian Journal for the Scholarship of Teaching and Learning* 6.2 (2015).

33. Robert B. Pippin, "Ways of Knowing," *The Point*, https://thepointmag.com/2014/criticism/ways-knowing.

34. By focusing, for example, on the connections between such capitalism and inequality, see Thomas Piketty, *Capital in the 21st Century* (Cambridge, MA: Harvard University Press, 2014).

35. Theodor W. Adorno, "Education after Auschwitz," in *Critical Models: Interventions and Catchwords*, trans. Henry W. Pickford (New York: Columbia University Press, 1998), 201.

36. Adorno, "Education after Auschwitz," 193, 95.

37. Hannah Arendt, "The Crisis in Education," in *Between Past and Future: Eight Exercises in Political Thought* (New York: Penguin, 2006), 191.

38. Stanley Cavell, *In Quest of the Ordinary: Lines of Skepticism and Romanticism* (Chicago: University of Chicago Press, 1994), 40.

39. See Cavell, *The Claim of Reason*, 19–28. For more on this point, see Shuster, "On the Ethical Basis of Language."

40. Cavell, *The Claim of Reason*, 28. Note that this affirmation of expressivity does not underscore any normative or naturalized understanding of expression: there are many ways in which expressivity might be "voiced"—and many divergent forms that expressivity might take.

41. *The World Viewed: Reflections on the Ontology of Film: Enlarged Edition* (Cambridge, MA: Harvard University Press, 1979), 132.

42. An important figure for this entire possibility is Walter Benjamin. See notably Walter Benjamin, *The Arcades Project* (Cambridge, MA: Harvard University Press, 1999); "On the Concept of History," in *Selected Writings*, vol. 4, ed. Howard Eiland and Michael W. Jennings (Cambridge, MA: Harvard University Press, 2002).

43. See Hubert Dreyfus, *Being-in-the-World: A Commentary on Heidegger's Being and Time, Division I* (Cambridge, MA: MIT Press, 1991), 69 and following.

44. On this latter point, see especially Theodor W. Adorno, *Minima Moralia* (London: Verso, 2005); J.M. Bernstein, *Adorno: Disenchantment and Ethics* (Cambridge: Cambridge University Press, 2001), 396–415. Alternatively, see the critiques in thinkers as diverse as Thoreau, Nietzsche, Heidegger, Hegel, Marx, Dewey, Sartre, and others.

45. Arendt, "The Crisis in Education," 193.

46. Austin, "A Plea for Excuses," 182.

47. Cavell, *The World Viewed*, 117.

WORKS CITED

Adorno, Theodor W. "Education after Auschwitz." In *Critical Models: Interventions and Catchwords*, translated by Henry W. Pickford, 191–204. New York: Columbia University Press, 1998.

——. *Gesammelte Schriften*. 20 vols. Frankfurt am Main: Suhrkamp Verlag, 1984.

——. "Late Capitalism or Industrial Society?" In *Can One Live after Auschwitz? A Philosophical Reader*, edited by Rolf Tiedemann, translated by Rodney Livingstone, 111–25. Palo Alto: Stanford University Press, 2003.

——. *Lectures on Negative Dialectics*. Edited by Rolf Tiedemann. Translated by Rodney Livingstone. Cambridge: Polity Press, 2008.

——. *Minima Moralia*. London: Verso, 2005.

——. *Negative Dialectics*. Translated by E.B. Ashton. New York: Continuum, 1973.

Arendt, Hannah. "The Crisis in Education." In *Between Past and Future: Eight Exercises in Political Thought*, 170–93. New York: Penguin, 2006.

———. "What Is Authority?" In *Between Past and Future*, 91–142. London: Penguin, 1968.

Austin, J.L. "A Plea for Excuses." In *Philosophical Papers*, 175–204. Oxford: Oxford University Press, 1979.

Benjamin, Walter. *The Arcades Project*. Cambridge, MA: Harvard University Press, 1999.

———. "On the Concept of History." In *Selected Writings*, vol. 4, edited by Howard Eiland and Michael W. Jennings, 389–400. Cambridge, MA: Harvard University Press, 2002.

Berman, Marshall. *All That Is Solid Melts into Air: The Experience of Modernity*. New York: Simon and Schuster, 1983.

Bernstein, J.M. *Adorno: Disenchantment and Ethics*. Cambridge: Cambridge University Press, 2001.

Cavell, Stanley. "The Availability of Wittgenstein's Later Philosophy." In *Must We Mean What We Say?* 44–73. Cambridge, MA: Harvard University Press, 2002.

———. *The Claim of Reason: Wittgenstein, Skepticism, Morality, and Tragedy*. Oxford: Oxford University Press, 1979.

———. "Emerson's Constitutional Amending." In *Emerson's Transcendental Etudes*, edited by David Justin Hodge, 192–215. Palo Alto: Stanford University Press, 2003.

———. *In Quest of the Ordinary: Lines of Skepticism and Romanticism*. Chicago: University of Chicago Press, 1994.

———. *This New Yet Unapproachable America: Lectures after Emerson after Wittgenstein*. Albuquerque, NM: Living Batch Press, 1989.

———. *The World Viewed: Reflections on the Ontology of Film: Enlarged Edition*. Cambridge, MA: Harvard University Press, 1979.

Cook, Deborah. *The Culture Industry Revisited: Theodor W. Adorno on Mass Culture*. Lanham, MD: Rowman & Littlefield, 1996.

Das, Veena. *Life and Words: Violence and the Descent into the Ordinary*. Berkeley: University of California Press, 2007.

Dreyfus, Hubert. *Being-in-the-World: A Commentary on Heidegger's Being and Time, Division I*. Cambridge, MA: MIT Press, 1991.

Emerson, Ralph Waldo. *The Essential Writings of Ralph Waldo Emerson*. New York: Modern Library, 2009.

Fain, Paul. "Rubio Changes Tune on Philosophers." *Chronicle of Higher Education*, March 29, 2018, https://www.insidehighered.com/quicktakes/2018/03/29/rubio-changes-tune-philosophers.

Freyenhagen, Fabian. "Adorno's Politics Theory and Praxis in Germany's 1960s." *Philosophy & Social Criticism* 40.9 (2014): 867–93.

———. *Adorno's Practical Philosophy: Living Less Wrongly*. Cambridge: Cambridge University Press, 2013.

Jaarsma, Ada S. "On Being Taught." *Canadian Journal for the Scholarship of Teaching and Learning* 6.2 (2015): 6.

Lorde, Audre. *Sister Outsider: Essays and Speeches*. New York: Crossing Press, 2012.

Marx, Karl. *The Marx-Engels Reader*. Edited by Robert C. Tucker. 2nd ed. New York: Norton, 1978.

Nietzsche, Friedrich W. *Thus Spoke Zarathustra*. Translated by Adrian Del Caro. Cambridge: Cambridge University Press, 2006.

Piketty, Thomas. *Capital in the 21st Century*. Cambridge, MA: Harvard University Press, 2014.

Pippin, Robert B. *Modernism as a Philosophical Problem: On the Dissatisfaction of European High Culture*. 2nd ed. Oxford: Blackwell, 1999.

———. "Ways of Knowing." *The Point*. https://thepointmag.com/2014/criticism/ways-knowing.

Shuster, Martin. "Adorno and Negative Theology." *Graduate Faculty Philosophy Journal* 37.1 (2015): 97–130.

———. *Autonomy after Auschwitz: Adorno, German Idealism, and Modernity*. Chicago: University of Chicago Press, 2014.

———. "Language and Loneliness: Arendt, Cavell, and Modernity." *International Journal of Philosophical Studies* 20.4 (2012): 473–97.

———. "Nothing to Know: The Epistemology of Moral Perfectionism in Adorno and Cavell." *Idealistic Studies* 44.1 (2015): 1–29.

———. "On the Ethical Basis of Language: Some Themes in Davidson, Cavell, and Levinas." *Journal for Cultural and Religious Theory* 14.2 (2015): 241–66.

———. "Rorty and (the Politics of) Love." *Graduate Faculty Philosophy Journal* 40.1 (2019): 65–78.

Taylor, Charles. *A Secular Age*. Cambridge, MA: Harvard University Press, 2007.

———. *Sources of the Self: The Making of the Modern Identity*. Cambridge, MA: Harvard University Press, 1989.

Weber, Max. "Politics as Vocation." In *From Max Weber: Essays in Sociology*, edited and translated by H.H. Gerth and C. Wright Mills, 77–129. London: Routledge, 1948.

———. *The Protestant Ethic and the Spirit of Capitalism: And Other Writings*. Translated by Peter Baehr and Gordon C. Wells. New York: Penguin, 2002.

———. "Science as Vocation." In *From Max Weber: Essays in Sociology*, edited and translated by H.H. Gerth and C. Wright Mills, 129–59. London: Routledge, 1948.

Wittgenstein, Ludwig. *Philosophical Investigations*. Translated by G.E.M. Anscombe. Upper Saddle River, NJ: Prentice Hall, 1958.

———. *Philosophical Occasions, 1912–1951*. Edited by James C. Klagge and Alfred Nordmann. Indianapolis: Hackett, 1993.

Pedagogy, Event, Risk

KYLE KINASCHUK

Introduction

Here is the main claim that I elaborate in this chapter[1]: if teaching is to occur at all, then pedagogy enters what Mary Louise Pratt calls a "contact zone"[2] with the event. This concept, "the event," is a key philosophical concern of this chapter. In my account, to teach or to be taught in the humanities classroom is to participate in unforeseen encounters with others, encounters that extend beyond what teachers can transmit and students are capable of learning on their own. The event provides a vocabulary for discussing moments when the bound- aries, the self-contained epistemic fields, of teachers and students become undone. Moreover, this argument draws upon an implicit understanding of "the event" that is at play in recent critiques of neoliberal models of education, models that are based upon "constructivist" or highly individualized accounts of teaching and learning.[3] Gert Biesta, for example, identifies such constructivist trends in higher education as complicit with unfortunate leanings toward what he describes as "learnification."[4] Learnification, Biesta explains, relegates the role of the teacher in the classroom to a mere resource, as students become self-sufficient learners and teachers become analogous to any other resource such as the internet or curricular texts.[5] By shifting the site of teaching from the activities of teachers to the construction of knowledge on the part of students, teachers become mere facilitators rather than pedagogues.[6] And so the very enterprise of "teaching" is at risk, at least on Biesta's diagnosis of higher education. I am persuaded by Biesta's account and seek, in this chapter, to explore more fully the riskiness of teaching. As I explore in the following sections, much is at stake in how we understand activities like "teaching" and "learning"—and, perhaps more pressingly for this chapter, how we understand the scholarly work that addresses teaching and learning, like the Scholarship of Teaching and Learning (SoTL); these stakes are all the higher because of increasing pressures from neoliberal forces on university classrooms.

It is important, first, to be clear about what I mean by the concept of the event. Looking in particular to Jacques Derrida and to contemporary readers of Derrida, I lay out an account of the event in which two aspects of pedagogy are of note: singularity and repetition.[7] By emphasizing the singular, or the entirely particular and unique, dynamics of pedagogy, as well as its repetitive form, I proffer an understanding of pedagogy that counters prevailing constructivist accounts of teaching and learning. As Derrida explains, this logic involves both "repetition *and* first time: this is perhaps the question of the event."[8] The concept of the event as a site of both newness and repetition offers an alternative to constructivist models of teaching and learning.

The Risks of Pedagogy

As I explore below, my reflections on teaching, learning, and SoTL are attuned to the riskiness of the pedagogical event. More specifically, there is one modality of risk, namely the risk of epistemic vulnerability, that becomes more salient when pedagogy is cast as an event. As Rachel Jones identifies in her chapter in this collection, the encounter or the event of pedagogy is intimately connected with the "existential and ontological vulnerability" of teachers and students, and this vulnerability is disproportionately distributed across classrooms and university spaces. When we take seriously the inequitable distributions of vulnerability, we are more able to recognize how prevailing institutional norms saturate (and often even dictate) the activities and interactions occurring within our classrooms. Consider, for example, how institutional norms such as whiteness, able-bodiedness, heteronormativity, and gender normativity are not "abstract" or solely "structural" but, instead, are lived out as somatic expressions of identity and selfhood. This movement from the abstract and structural to the somatic is to read "institutional norms as somatic norms," as Sara Ahmed writes.[9] Such norms distribute the affective, emotional, and intellectual labour of classroom activities asymmetrically. And this asymmetrical distribution then acts as a feedback loop, reinforcing the very sorts of inequalities that give rise to such disproportional burdens of labour: norms such as whiteness fade into the background, permitting certain bodies to be more at ease than other bodies to either participate (and voluntarily enter into the riskiness of learning) or to opt out of difficult conversations (and voluntarily bolster a sense of self-sufficiency). A classroom is much more risky, in other words, for some bodies than for others, and this is why the event of pedagogy is an essentially ethical matter: it's of great ethical import, on this account of classrooms, that teachers deploy what we as contributors to this edited collection are calling "dissonant methods," pedagogical methods that affirm the vulnerability of students while undercutting and minimizing the asymmetries at work in classroom encounters.

A pedagogy of the event that affirms the unexpected, such as the ludic or the playful or simply the surprising, easily lapses into a logic that ignores vulnerability all together. It is all too common, after all, for theorists of education and social life to presuppose a "universal subject," one that is anterior to material, embodied life. Such accounts foreclose negotiating the classroom as a site constituted by the unstable and emergent scales of what Jasbir Puar calls "conviviality." Conviviality casts "categories such as race, gender, and sexuality as events—as encounters—rather than as entities or attributes of the subject."[10] To think conviviality in the classroom, then, is to hold onto the word's usual meaning of being in good company, of living with, and sharing a table and space together. And yet conviviality, as Puar notes, "does not lead to a politics of the universal or inclusive common...[but] rather the futurity enabled through the open materiality of bodies as a Place to Meet."[11] The classroom is not like most places where bodies meet, though. As teachers, we are responsible, to a certain degree, for coordinating the very shape, tempo, and constitution of *how* bodies will meet in the classroom. So here are the difficult questions that arise from such reflections on vulnerability: Do I veer too closely to underscoring the unfair and harmful inequalities of classrooms when I make the case for the contingency of pedagogy-as-event? After all, it is the contingencies of embodied experiences that are, in part, in need of shifting through pedagogical methods. How might we affirm the openness to the new and the unexpected, as I hope to do with an account of pedagogy as evental, given that some bodies enjoy privilege through pedagogical encounters while others experience the exhaustion that comes from living out the uneven scales of vulnerability within classrooms?

It might be helpful, in thinking through these questions, to recall that these reflections are at odds with dominant frameworks of education, learning, and pedagogy. While I want to emphasize the relationality of the event, it is crucial to my argument that I do not fall into paradigms of learning that underscore or exacerbate highly inequitable experiences within classrooms and universities more broadly. As one example of this latter possibility, I turn briefly to the influential work of Martha C. Nussbaum, who casts pedagogy in the terms of sympathetic growth and imagination. It is the reader, in particular, who is the learner on Nussbaum's account. In *Not For Profit: Why Democracy Needs the Humanities*, Nussbaum argues, "Instruction in literature and the arts can cultivate sympathy in many ways, through engagement with many different works of literature, music, fine art, and dance."[12] Literature, as in Nussbaum's reading of Theodor Fontane's tragic *Effi Briest*, functions as an "exercise in learning."[13] Readers learn from a certain voyeurism of reading; they are cast as spectators in order to expand their imagination. And the loss or the violence experienced by others is recuperated—implicitly or explicitly—as a lesson of sorts for the reader-student. This recuperation is essential to the liberal tradition more generally, perhaps best hyperbolized in Adam Smith's sympathetic occupation of the dead: "we sympathize even with the dead...putting ourselves in their situations, and...lodging, if I may be allowed to say so, our own living souls in their inanimated bodies, and thence conceiving what would be our emotions in this case."[14]

In these literary transpositions of the reading self onto the other, the liberal sympathetic imagination annihilates real differences, or the alterity, of the other.[15] Sympathy might be better described as an imposition, in other words, than as virtuous compassion: the reader seeks *to be* the other rather than be *with* the other. In the words of two key theorists of relationality, Saidiya Hartman and Vinciane Despret, this mode of reading simply reproduces a "grammar of violence"[16] that "squats in the other."[17] Likewise, Édouard Glissant describes this kind of sympathy: "I thus am able to conceive of the opacity of the other for me, without reproach for my opacity for him. To feel in solidarity with him or to build with him or to like what he does, it is not necessary for me to grasp him. It is not necessary to become the other (to become other) nor to 'make him in my image.'"[18] There is a cruelty to the gestures of sympathy, on such accounts, and as we acknowledge this cruelty, we can join Michel Foucault in seeking to "not rest content to be merely one of the forms of likeness."[19] This phrasing from Foucault gets to the heart of what's at stake in pedagogy: we risk capitalizing upon the alterity (or really real differences) of another when we describe reading and other pedagogical activities solely in terms of "likeness." But, while a certain sympathy or empathy adheres to the promise that the student might come to understand another, there are other modes of relating to others. These modes proffer the conditions of possibility for displacing *likeness* with the unexpected, and for replacing sympathetic imagination with the event.

The Event and the Conditions of Possibility for SoTL

The stakes and implications of defining pedagogy in terms of the event offer an alternative vocabulary to constructivist accounts of teaching and learning. Michael K. Potter confirms constructivism as the predominant pedagogical philosophy in the Scholarship of Teaching and Learning,[20] and so in this section, I reflect on the challenges and possibilities in my account of evental pedagogy in the context of SoTL. SoTL is an institutionalized area of research that first materialized when Ernest L. Boyer, the president of the Carnegie Foundation for the Advancement of Teaching, published his report, *Scholarship Reconsidered: Priorities of the Professoriate*, in 1990.[21] Recall that in constructivist accounts of learning, the teacher merely aids the student in the process of learning; rather than teaching the student, the teacher (who is not really occupying the role of teacher) coaxes the student through dialogue toward an immanent moment that was already possible. The inward movement toward an epistemic accretion of knowledge is more a restoration of knowledge's possibility, on this understanding, rather than the arrival of radically new knowledge: it is not an encounter with impossible or difficult knowledge but rather the fulfilment of latent potential. As Plato illustrates when Socrates plays midwife for Theaetetus in *Theaetetus*, "So begin again, Theaetetus, and try to say what knowledge is. And don't on any account tell me that you can't."[22] What is especially significant here is that, at each site of knowledge acquisition, the possibility of epistemic transmission is presupposed from its inception, so much so that one is merely attaining knowledge that already exists and dwells within a sphere of possibility. Hence, one is not entirely being taught from the outside. The act of receiving a lesson equates either to recalling what one already knows through Socratic midwifery or relegating knowledge to a calculable resource accessible to anyone through their own capacities.

As an alternative to constructivism, we can begin to write of pedagogy as evental. But what challenges does this pose to the methods and commitments of SoTL? I want to stress my own interests in an enterprise like the scholarly, collaborative, and exploratory scholarship on teaching and learning. Yet I also want to make the case for an approach to SoTL that makes use of other logics than those of constructivism. In order to advance this case, I make use of the Derridean concept of the event, which I lay out in more detail below. I turn to SoTL, and then reflect on the conditions of possibility for scholarly work on teaching and learning that is attuned to the riskiness and ethical import of the event.

"The event" is a concept that cannot be readily generalized. Derrida reserves the concept of the event, for example, for those scenarios or encounters that have the following specific qualities: they are unforeseeable, singular, and irruptive; they cannot be subsumed into an overarching linear narrative, nor summed up by way of a delimited outcome; they occur through dynamics that fall, as if "vertically" or out of the sky, that cannot be appropriated by "any law, norm, determinative judgement, or technoscience."[23] The event, Derrida explains, cannot be anticipated: it arrives, without being calculated ahead of time or for that matter calculated after the fact. "[T]he event as event, as absolute surprise," Derrida writes, "must fall on me. Why? Because if it doesn't fall on me, it means that I see it coming that there's a horizon of expectation. Horizontally, I see it coming, I fore-see it, I fore-say it, and the event is that which can be said [*dit*] but never predicted [*prédit*]."[24] The event shatters any field of prediction, program, or economy of expectation in its singularity. But, Derrida continues, the event also grates against the blunt rapidity of repetition:

> When I welcome a visitor, when I receive the visitation of an unexpected visitor, it must be a unique experience each and every time for it to be a unique, unpredictable, singular, and irreplaceable event. But at the same time, the repetition of the event must be presupposed, from the threshold of the house and from the arrival of the irreplaceable. "I welcome you," means, "I promise to welcome you again." It will not do to greet someone saying, "it's all right this time, but..." There must already be a promise of repetition.[25]

There's a seeming contradiction that animates Derrida's understanding of the event: the event is singular, yet imminently repeatable. In one of Derrida's earliest engagements with the event, he writes of iterability as etymologically linked to both the Latin word *iter* (again) and the Sanskrit word *itara* (other).[26] This linkage is, in part, where the riskiness of the event lies: the very capacity for repetition threatens the singularity of the event, erasing its contingency, and yet the horizon of the event is one of iterability, such that it can happen again and again. There is a twofold riskiness here: first, the risk, described above, in which the embodied specificities and differences are elided in the name of "likeness" or empathy; second, the risk that I explore more fully in this section in which repetition becomes machinic, substituting the irreplaceably singular dimensions of the event with a generalized rote set of reiterations.

Derrida helps us glimpse a certain uncanny temporality to how events play out: events are out of sync with their own happening. And this poses a fascinating challenge to scholarly projects that seek to do justice to the "hap," as Sara Ahmed calls it, of pedagogical encounters where "the hap might embrace what happens, but it also works toward a world in which things can happen in alternative ways."[27] In the terms that Derrida tends to use, there is an after-an-eventness, or *Nachträglichkeit*, which engenders a repetition of the event—one that indefinitely prolongs the afterlife of an event. It could be that SoTL, in seeking to adhere fully to the exchanges between teachers and students, is more accurately described as adhering to the after-life of teaching.

Iterability, Geoffrey Bennington explains, "may affect the event from the start, dividing its uniqueness and giving rise to the possibility of different versions and accounts of the 'same' event, but iterability also entails alteration and difference, so that something new, a new event, takes place in every account of the event."[28] And so there is a meta-conceptual challenge that emerges from this discussion, which has to do with the ways in which the event resists its own identification *as* an event. The event, put in another way, resists the very category of "singularity," because the singular is not a template or an example or a general law. If the event is to remain absolutely singular, then the event cannot be subsumed by a generalized category of the event. So how might we engage in scholarly representations of teaching and learning in ways that heed the lessons of Derrida's event?

As a way to engage with these challenges, I return to the work of Biesta with which I began this chapter. The event occurs at the threshold of the contradictions and impasses of curricular design and institutional demands, on the one side, and the contingencies of teaching, on the other side. In more concrete terms, the act of teaching cannot solely depend upon objective models that are then implemented in classrooms as if it were possible to replicate the exact same pedagogical encounters again and again. While teaching requires work in advance through lesson plans and their numerous apparatuses, each lesson plan leads to divergent responses that play out differently each time they are put into practice and play in the classroom. And this is why to be taught, to receive the gift of teaching as Biesta puts it, might be conceptualized as an event.

The event, first and foremost, acknowledges that to teach and to learn necessitates negotiating the world with others, that is, inhabiting spaces collaboratively with an openness toward the uncertain as well as the opaque.[29] To invoke some Derridean phrasing, there is a promise at play in teaching that involves a "yes before the yes": a commitment to a certain openness simply by inhabiting a space with one another. As Derrida might put it, the event always remains "to come," rather than occurring as calculated or expected. A pedagogy of the event, then, is a "pedagogy without a project,"[30] one that demands responsibility to the shifting dynamics and circumstances of the classroom. Evental pedagogy is akin to what Erin Manning calls "a pragmatics of the useless,"[31] which affirms not knowing in advance where thought might take us and staves off impositions of value from the outside.

There is a difference, after all, between an event or a future that is to come and an event or a future that is never to come. The event that never comes is not an event; rather, it is death—what Derrida might describe as absolute transcendence, in which time is not out of joint, but out of time. A future without a future, we could say, is empty and unscathed from time—a time without time. It is because the event is to come—arriving unpredictably, tearing the fabric of possibility, and forcing us to respond suddenly—that we have the chance to repeat things anew.

And so, an evental pedagogy does not feign mastery over the pedagogical field, as if teachers could act as sovereigns over the event and its distribution in classrooms. In fact, it is the very converse that is true, and this is where SoTL becomes a pressing endeavour when disentangled from constructivism. As I have argued elsewhere, the contingencies of the classroom are often inter-related with the design choices of the instructor and the institution.[32] According to disability studies, there is an imperative to move beyond accommodation models that aim to incorporate the individual into existing structures in favour of universal design principles in the classroom that can attend to the ways in which design choices shape and orient bodies by tacitly reproducing sites of privilege in seemingly innocuous ways.[33] This is to emphasize "material justice over nominal formal equality,"[34] as Aimi Hamraie writes.

An evental pedagogy, as Biesta points out, can only prepare for the coming, the arrival, of teaching: "This means that deconstructive inventiveness can consist only in opening, in uncloseting, destabilizing foreclosionary struc-tures so as to allow for the passage toward the other. But one should not forget that one does not make the other come. One lets it come by preparing for its coming. Education, in short, therefore, prepares for the incalculable."[35] Above all, to recognize the evental nature of the classroom is to remain committed to a future of living responsibly in relation to whatever might arrive, that is, to remain vigilant and accountable to not only the unpredictable moments that happen in the classroom but also to constantly revise and attend to institutional and instructional design choices that participate in and work against systematic modes of oppression.

Scholars of pedagogy, teaching, and learning are, ourselves, accountable in ways that open us up to the surprise of the event while we design our classroom spaces and our curriculum. Here is the crux of Derrida's account of the event: the event arrives, but the event also forces us to act. Pheng Cheah explains, "This impossible coming of the other is not utopian. It is a force of precipitation that is experienced as an eruption within the order of presence and that in turn forces the experiencing subject to act."[36] The event, or the arrival of real difference, disturbs and disrupts the order of presence. And on Derrida's account, this disruption exceeds the subject's capacity to act; it undercuts the "rational," "self-contained," and "autonomous" subject's ability to govern and master itself. By undermining the separation between passivity and activity, the event precedes us and comes from the radically other, yet it still forces us to respond through what Derrida describes as a passive activity. Derrida argues, "If an event worthy of the name is to happen, it must, beyond all mastery, affect a passivity. It must touch a vulnerability that is exposed, without absolute immunity."[37] Here is where the riskiness of vulnerability, described above, is the very crux of the event of teaching and learning. The event arrives, but the event addresses each of us differently. As Elizabeth Povinelli reminds us, "The actual world does not address all of us in the same way."[38] Just as vulnerability is one of the most pressing challenges for pedagogues, vulnerability is also what is most at stake in the event. When we conceptualize teaching and learning in terms of the event, we are more fully able to resist the logic that assumes a "universal subject" that transcends the particular embodied dimensions of lived experience.

The event of teaching would not occur if the dangers of risk were abolished. And yet, following Rachel Jones, I want to emphasize that it is "crucial to avoid a false opposition between critical pedagogy and 'safe spaces.'"[39] In other words, a pedagogy of the event is in no way in alliance with calls for so-called free speech, which completely efface social difference, willfully ignore ongoing sites of oppression, and presuppose all bodies have the means and desire to be rendered intelligible within liberal discourses of rationality and debate. Above all, to recognize the evental nature of the classroom is to remain committed to a future of living on responsibly to whatever might arrive, that is, to remain vigilant and accountable to not only the unpredictable moments that happen in the classroom but also to constantly revise and attend to institutional and instructional design choices that participate in systemic modes of oppression. Nonetheless, there is an attendant risk that arrives on the scene here, for to revise the university and its design choices prolongs the originary violence of the university as a colonial institution. While it remains vital to minimize violence from within the university, it is equally important to look beyond the university to enact what Tavleen Purewal calls "small decolonial acts that function within the university and take knowledge beyond it, turn the inside-out."[40] An evental pedagogy, then, might even be said to be quasi-evental from this perspective. The ongoing work we are left with is how to defy a certain fetishization of possibility and risk in the classroom, which is felt differentially through and through, by creating provisional sites of persistence and survival from within the ruins of the university all the while reserving opacity, silence, and recalcitrance to the university.

NOTES

1. I'm grateful for the detailed commentary on this chapter that I received from Kit Dobson, Rohan Ghatage, Henry Ivry, and Tavleen Purewal. I'm especially grateful to Ada Jaarsma for her extensive, patient, and thoughtful engagement. I'm also thankful for Ada Jaarsma and Kit Dobson's invitation to participate in the Dissonant Methods Workshop in Banff in 2016, where the earliest form of this chapter took shape. The conversations that occurred in Banff were immensely helpful. I also extend my thanks to the anonymous reviewers at the University of Alberta Press for their insightful commentaries.

2. Mary Louise Pratt, "Arts of the Contact Zone," *Modern Language Association* (1991).

3. While constructivism certainly cannot be homogenized, and spans a range of irreducible interlocutors such as John Dewey, Ernst von Glasersfeld, Lev Vygotsky, and Jean Piaget, constructionism, nevertheless, privileges the learner's capacity to actively construct knowledge on their own terms by fostering the conditions under which students can generate their own knowledge. See Virginia Richardson, "Constructivist Pedagogy," *Teachers College Record* 105.9 (2003); Wolff-Michael Roth, *Possibility: At the Limits of the Constructivist Metaphor* (New York: Springer, 2011); Ari Sutinen, "Constructivism and Education: Education as an Interpretative Transformational Process," *Studies in the Philosophy of Education* 27 (2007); and Laurance J. Splitter, "Authenticity and Constructivism in Education," *Studies in the Philosophy of Education* 28 (2009).

4. Gert Biesta, "Receiving the Gift of Teaching: From 'Learning From' to 'Being Taught By,'" *Studies in Philosophy and Education* 32.5 (2013).

5. As I examine in more detail below, "constructivism" is sometimes described as Socratic, or maieutic. Sharon Todd helps draw out the limitations of this understanding of pedagogy: "The maieutic method erases the significance of the Other and claims that learning is a recovery contained within the I, rather than a disruption of the I provoked by the Other in a moment of sociality." See Sharon Todd, *Learning from the Other: Levinas, Psychoanalysis, and Ethical Possibilities in Education* (New York: SUNY Press, 2003), 30.

6. In this way, this chapter continues the work I commenced with Ada Jaarsma and Lin Xing in "Kierkegaard, Despair, and the Possibility of Education: Teaching Existentialism Existentially," *Studies in Philosophy and Education* 35.5 (2016), which lays

the groundwork for much of the thinking here concerning the event and the pedagogical.

7. While there are other philosophers and traditions that theorize "the event," this chapter is most concerned with Derrida's thinking, heeding Michael Naas's suggestion that "the event...is what was always at the heart of Derrida's thought." See *Derrida From Now On* (New York: Fordham University Press, 2008), 29.

8. Jacques Derrida, *Specters of Marx: The State of Debt, the Work of Mourning, and the New International*, trans. Peggy Kamuf (New York: Routledge, 1994), 10.

9. Sara Ahmed, *On Being Included: Racism and Diversity in Institutional Life* (Durham, NC: Duke University Press, 2012), 38.

10. Jasbir K. Puar, "Prognosis Time: Towards a Geopolitics of Affect, Debility, and Capacity," *Women and Performance: A Journal of Feminist Theory* 19.2 (2009): 168.

11. Puar, 168.

12. Martha C. Nussbaum, *Not For Profit: Why Democracy Needs the Humanities* (Princeton, NJ: Princeton University Press, 2010).

13. Martha C. Nussbaum, *Political Emotions: Why Love Matters for Justice* (Cambridge, MA: Harvard University Press, 2013), 141.

14. Adam Smith, *The Theory of Moral Sentiments* (New York: Cosimo, 2007): 4–5.

15. We could differentiate between "sympathy" and "empathy" here. Jane Bennett, for example, convincingly rehabilitates sympathy as onto-sympathy through a vitalist and materialist reading that disavows the liberal notion of sympathy as "a subjective emotion or sentiment." Bennett understands sympathy as an "impersonal mesh of affiliations between natural bodies." See Jane Bennett, "Vegetal Life and Onto-Sympathy," in *Entangled Worlds: Religion, Science and New Materialisms*, ed. Catherine Keller and Mary-Jane Rubenstein (New York: Fordham University Press, 2017), 91. On Bennett's account, we can understand "empathy" as a synonym for the over-reach of liberal sentiments ("squatting in the other," as Despret puts it); in contrast, sympathy seems to hold more possibility as a relational term that respects or even affirms dissonance.

16. Saidiya Hartman, "Venus in Two Acts," *Small Axe* 26.12.2 (2008): 4.

17. Vinciane Despret, "The Body We Care For: Figures of Anthropo-zoo-genesis," *Body & Society* 10.2–3 (2004): 128.

18. Édouard Glissant, *Poetics of Relation*, trans. Betsy Wing (Ann Arbor: University of Michigan Press, 1997), 193.

19. Michel Foucault, *The Order of Things: An Archeology of the Human Sciences* (London and New York: Routledge, 2002), 26.

20. Michael K. Potter, "Constructivism in the Shadow of a Dead God," *International Journal for the Scholarship of Teaching and Learning* 7.1 (2013): 3.

21. For an extensive and incisive engagement with SoTL that does not merely identify SoTL as a site of "learnification" but also engages its ideological and pedagogical presuppositions, see Ada Jaarsma, "On Being Taught," *The Canadian Journal for the Scholarship of Teaching and Learning* 6.2 (2016).

22. Plato, *Theaetetus*, trans. M.J. Levett, rev. by Myles Burnyeat (Indianapolis: Hackett, 1990), 271.

23. Jacques Derrida, *Rogues: Two Essays on Reason*, trans. Pascale-Ann Brault and Michael Naas (Stanford: Stanford University Press, 2005), 148.

24. Jacques Derrida, "A Certain Impossible Possibility of Saying the Event," trans. Gila Walker, *Critical Inquiry* 33.2 (2007): 451.

25. Derrida, "A Certain Impossible Possibility," 453.

26. Jacques Derrida, "Signature Event Context," in *Margins of Philosophy*, trans. Alan Bass (Chicago: University of Chicago Press, 1982), 315.

27. Sara Ahmed, *The Promise of Happiness* (Durham, NC: Duke University Press, 2010), 223.

28. Geoffrey Bennington, "In the Event," in *Derrida's Legacies: Literature and Philosophy*, ed. Robert Eaglestone and Simon Glendinning (London: Routledge, 2009), 33.

29. See Rachel Jones's chapter in this book.

30. Anne O'Byrne, "Pedagogy Without A Project: Arendt and Derrida on Teaching, Responsibility, and Revolution," *Studies in Philosophy and Education* 24 (2005): 406.

31. Erin Manning, "10 Propositions for a Radical Pedagogy, or How to Rethink Value," *Inflexions* 8 (2015): 206.

32. Jaarsma, Kinaschuk, and Xing, "Kierkegaard, Despair, and the Possibility of Education," 455.

33. Ada S. Jaarsma, "Design, Disability and Play: The Animal Politics of Education," *Gender and Education* 28.2 (2016).

34. Aimi Hamraie, *Building Access: Universal Design and the Politics of Disability* (Minneapolis: Minnesota University Press, 2017), 260.

35. Gert Biesta, "Deconstruction, Justice, and the Vocation of Education," *Counterpoints* 323 (2009): 35.

36. Pheng Cheah, "Non-Dialectical Materialism," in *New Materialisms: Ontology, Agency, and Politics*, ed. Diana Coole and Samantha Frost (Durham, NC: Duke University Press, 2010), 76.

37. Derrida, *Rogues*, 152.

38. Elizabeth Povinelli, *Economies of Abandonment: Social Belonging and Endurance in Late Liberalism* (Durham, NC: Duke University Press, 2011), 138.

39. See Rachel Jones's chapter in this book.

40. Tavleen Purewal, "The Beyond of the University: Decolonizing Humanities Pedagogy" (paper, Centre for Integrative Anti-Racism Studies Decolonizing Conference, Ontario Institute for Studies in Education of the University of Toronto, November 9, 2018).

WORKS CITED

Ahmed, Sara. *On Being Included: Racism and Diversity in Institutional Life*. Durham, NC: Duke University Press, 2012.

———. *The Promise of Happiness*. Durham, NC: Duke University Press, 2010.

Bennett, Jane. "Vegetal Life and Onto-Sympathy." In *Entangled Worlds: Religion, Science and New Materialisms*, edited by Catherine Keller and Mary-Jane Rubenstein, 89–110. New York: Fordham University Press, 2017.

Bennington, Geoffrey. "In the Event." In *Derrida's Legacies: Literature and Philosophy*, edited by Robert Eaglestone and Simon Glendinning, 26–35. London: Routledge, 2009.

Biesta, Gert. "Deconstruction, Justice, and the Vocation of Education." *Counterpoints* 323 (2009): 15–37.

———. "Receiving the Gift of Teaching: From 'Learning From' to 'Being Taught By.'" *Studies in Philosophy and Education* 32.5 (2013): 449–61.

Cheah, Pheng. "Non-Dialectical Materialism." In *New Materialisms: Ontology, Agency, and Politics*, edited by Diana Coole and Samantha Frost, 70–91. Durham, NC: Duke University Press, 2010.

Derrida, Jacques. "A Certain Impossible Possibility of Saying the Event," translated by Gila Walker. *Critical Inquiry* 33.2 (2007): 441–61.

———. *Rogues: Two Essays on Reason*. Translated by Pascale-Ann Brault and Michael Naas. Stanford: Stanford University Press, 2005.

———. "Signature Event Context." In *Margins of Philosophy*, translated by Alan Bass, 309–30. Chicago: University of Chicago Press, 1982.

———. *Specters of Marx: The State of Debt, the Work of Mourning, and the New International*. Translated by Peggy Kamuf. New York: Routledge, 1994.

Despret, Vinciane. "The Body We Care For: Figures of Anthropo-zoo-genesis." *Body & Society* 10.2–3 (2004): 111–34.

Foucault, Michel. *The Order of Things: An Archeology of the Human Sciences*. London and New York: Routledge, 2002.

Glissant, Édouard. *Poetics of Relation*. Translated by Betsy Wing. Ann Arbor: University of Michigan Press, 1997.

Hamraie, Aimi. *Building Access: Universal Design and the Politics of Disability*. Minneapolis: Minnesota University Press, 2017.

Hartman, Saidiya. "Venus in Two Acts." *Small Axe* 26.12.2 (2008): 1–14.

Jaarsma, Ada S. "Design, Disability and Play: The Animal Politics of Education." *Gender and Education* 28.2 (2016): 195–212.

———. "On Being Taught." *The Canadian Journal for the Scholarship of Teaching and Learning* 6.2 (2016): 1–12.

Jaarsma, Ada S., Kyle Kinaschuk, and Lin Xing. "Kierkegaard, Despair, and the Possibility of Education: Teaching Existentialism Existentially." *Studies in Philosophy and Education* 35.5 (2016): 445–61.

Manning, Erin. "10 Propositions for a Radical Pedagogy, or How to Rethink Value." *Inflexions* 8 (2015): 202–10.

Naas, Michael. *Derrida From Now On*. New York: Fordham University Press, 2008.

Nussbaum, Martha C. *Not For Profit: Why Democracy Needs the Humanities*. Princeton, NJ: Princeton University Press, 2010.

———. *Political Emotions: Why Love Matters for Justice*. Cambridge, MA: Harvard University Press, 2013.

O'Byrne, Anne. "Pedagogy Without A Project: Arendt and Derrida on Teaching, Responsibility, and Revolution." *Studies in Philosophy and Education* 24 (2005): 389–409.

Plato. *Theaetetus*. Translated by M.J. Levett. Revised by Myles Burnyeat. Indianapolis: Hackett, 1990.

Potter, Michael K. "Constructivism in the Shadow of a Dead God." *International Journal for the Scholarship of Teaching and Learning* 7.1 (2013): 1–12.

Povinelli, Elizabeth. *Economies of Abandonment: Social Belonging and Endurance in Late Liberalism*. Durham, NC: Duke University Press, 2011.

Pratt, Mary Louise. "Arts of the Contact Zone." *Modern Language Association* (1991): 33–40.

Puar, Jasbir K. "Prognosis Time: Towards a Geopolitics of Affect, Debility, and Capacity." *Women and Performance: A Journal of Feminist Theory* 19.2 (2009): 161–72.

Purewal, Tavleen. "The Beyond of the University: Decolonizing Humanities Pedagogy." Paper presented at the Centre for Integrative Anti-Racism Studies Decolonizing Conference, Ontario Institute for Studies in Education of the University of Toronto, November 9, 2018.

Richardson, Virginia. "Constructivist Pedagogy." *Teachers College Record* 105.9 (2003): 1623–40.

Roth, Wolff-Michael. *Passibility: At the Limits of the Constructivist Metaphor*. New York: Springer, 2011.

Smith, Adam. *The Theory of Moral Sentiments*. New York: Cosimo, 2007.

Splitter, Laurance J. "Authenticity and Constructivism in Education." *Studies in the Philosophy of Education* 28 (2009): 135–51.

Sutinen, Ari. "Constructivism and Education: Education as an Interpretative Transformational Process." *Studies in the Philosophy of Education* 27 (2007): 1–14.

Todd, Sharon. *Learning from the Other: Levinas, Psychoanalysis, and Ethical Possibilities in Education*. New York: SUNY Press, 2003.

When the "Event" Happens

KATHY CAWSEY

KYLE KINASCHUK'S CHAPTER IN THIS VOLUME introduces us to
the Derridean concept of the "event" in teaching—of "evental pedagogy."
Teaching, he writes, is dependent upon the unanticipated, the unexpected,
the undecidable, the aporetic, and the radically other. This is a scary thought.
It means, on day one of term, that when I walk into the classroom, my hands
shake, my armpits sweat, and I am terrified—*every single time*—that this time,
the magic won't happen, the teaching won't work. Teaching always runs the risk
of failure. It also, more problematically, incorporates the possibility of violence,
an opening up toward what is other, uncertain, and contingent. Kyle adds that
this violence is asymmetrical, as not every body inhabits space in the same
manner; or reads texts in the same way; or comes to the classroom with the
same history. This situation creates a problem for teachers: if we are to embrace
an evental pedagogy, a pedagogical method that is exciting, opening, new, and
invigorating, we necessarily run the risk of violence. And that violence will fall
disproportionately on the most vulnerable bodies in our classroom. My contri-
bution to this volume is a story of one such dissonant moment, one such event,
that happened to me. I will narrate how the philosophical ideas in Kyle's article
turned into reality—a reality that crashed into the problem of violence, vulnerability, and bodies that other articles in this volume address.

The Event

The context of my story is Dalhousie University, Halifax, Nova Scotia, in February of 2015. In December of 2014, two months previously, the Canadian Broadcasting Company (CBC) had run a news story showing screenshots taken from a private Facebook group called the "Class of DDS (Dalhousie Dentistry School) 2015 Gentlemen."[1] The screenshots contained extremely misogynistic and violent posts, some of which were about women in the class, and one of which was posted twenty-five years to the day that Marc Lépine killed fourteen women at L'École Polytechnique in Montreal in what became known as the Montreal Massacre, as many media outlets would later point out. The story was all over the media, both traditional and social media, both because of the nature of the incident, coming as it did in a year that had seen the Jian Ghomeshi (a CBC radio host who was accused of sexual assault) and Bill Cosby scandals, and because of the nature of the participants involved, professional men who would someday have access to powerful drugs. As one journalist commented, the story "had legs," and kept going weeks and months after the initial incident. Dalhousie's name was dragged through the mud, and various groups—feminist, academic, and professional groups—accused Richard Florizone, Dal's president, and his administration, of a range of things, including fostering rape culture, protecting misogynists, and covering up previous incidents. University applications plummeted even in departments that had nothing to do with dentistry. In a controversial move, Dalhousie chose to deal with the incident through a restorative justice process, rather than through more traditional methods of punishment, such as expulsion, or the creation of permanent barriers for the men to prevent them from entering the dentistry profession or actively practising dentistry.[2] Many people decried this path of action, others defended it, and the furor went on.

By February, the media uproar had somewhat subsided, but the scandal was still very much on the minds of members of the Dalhousie community. I was teaching a third-year class on Geoffrey Chaucer's *Canterbury Tales*, written in the late 1380s or early 1390s. The class had reached "The Wife of Bath's Tale," a tale I have taught every year since I began teaching. The tale tells the story of a knight of King Arthur's court who is out riding one day. He sees a maiden walking by a river. He rapes her. The royal court convicts him and condemns him to death, but the women of the court ask to have the sentence commuted. The queen then sends him on a quest to find out "what women want." The knight goes on the quest and learns that what women really want is "sovereignty." Then he is forced himself to marry—and thus sleep with—the ugly old woman who gave him the answer. This is a clear reversal of roles, since the knight is essentially "raped" himself (in the only way medieval people thought it was possible to rape a man). His cry makes that clear: "Take all my goods and let my body go!"—the usual cry of somebody about to be raped. In bed, on the night of their marriage, the ugly old woman gives him a choice between having her beautiful and unfaithful, or old and faithful. He wallows and wails and finally says, "choose yourself," whereupon she decides to be that impossible creature, at least according to medieval anti-feminist literature—both beautiful *and* faithful.

The tale usually starts a pretty good discussion about gender, rape, women's rights, fairness, and the difference between medieval times and today.

In February 2015, though, it was different.

In February of 2015, when talking about the ending of the tale, I found myself saying, "So does anyone object to the fact that at the end of the tale the rapist gets the beautiful girl, and goes on to a successful career in dentistry?"

I realized, at that moment, *mid-sentence*, that the responses to Dalhousie's choice to go with "restorative justice" closely paralleled both the common student responses *and* the scholarly responses to "The Wife of Bath's Tale." The event of the Dal Dentistry scandal had erupted into the middle of a medieval tale, into the middle of a lecture that, by this point in my career, I had down pretty pat. Moreover, thinking about it in the days and weeks afterward, I came to the conclusion that one's response to both situations—both "The Wife of Bath's Tale" and the Dal Dentistry scandal—was necessarily conditioned by one's previously held, ingrained assumptions and beliefs about whether misogynists or rapists could ever really, fundamentally, change.

Rape in Medieval Times

Chaucer wrote *The Canterbury Tales*, and "The Wife of Bath's Tale" in particular, in a highly charged historical context. The legal crime of rape was changing in the 1380s. Part of the problem for us, at this historical distance, is that it is very hard for historians and literary historians to know precisely what the crime actually was in any given specific case. The Latin word "*raptus*," and the Anglo-Norman word "*ravyse*," *could* mean what we think of as "rape"—forced, nonconsensual sex—but the words also had the broader meaning of abduction or kidnapping. Chaucer himself, notoriously, was "released of the rape of Cecily Chaumpaigne" in 1380—from "*omnimodas acciones tam de raptu meo tam de aliqua alia re vel causa*"[3]—but, since the case was settled out of court, we do not know whether he actually forced Ms. Chaumpaigne to have sex, or abducted her, or, on the other hand, was falsely accused of doing either one.[4] (This ambiguity was rather comforting to Chaucerians of the first part of the last century, as well

35

as to many students, who—as with Sir Thomas Malory a hundred years later, another well-loved author accused of rape—have trouble acknowledging that one of their favourite authors could possibly be a rapist.) Whatever the actual events of the case were, we can at least be sure that Chaucer himself would have been hyper-aware of the significance of the debate in the 1380s over what constituted rape.

Because the law was changing. Up until 1275, according to Glanvill's laws and statutes, legal action for rape had to be initiated by the wronged woman, who "was expected to raise the hue, exhibit her torn garments and her bleeding to the local law officers, and prosecute the offender before the royal justices in eyre at the earliest opportunity."[5] Punishment was blinding or castration. In 1275, the first Statute of Westminster changed the law so that the Crown, rather than the raped woman herself, could prosecute.[6] Ten years later, the Second Statute of Westminster introduced the death penalty for a convicted rapist. Actual conviction, however, was rare, whether because the accused got off on a technicality, or because the defendant financially compensated or married the victim and the case would be dropped. One hundred years later, when Chaucer was writing, rape or *raptus* had changed from a violent assault against a particular woman to a property crime against the family. The extremes of punishment—castration, blinding, or the death penalty—were not being used by juries who were less harsh if it became evident that the woman consented, either at the time or afterwards (by "rewriting" the narrative of her rape as a narrative of marriage). The perception was that kidnapping or *raptus* had become a way for a consensual couple to elope against the wishes of the woman's parents, since the so-called rapist would have to marry the woman to save her honour, and because she would not otherwise be marriageable. The focus of the law was shifting: rather than protecting a woman's physical being from assault, the law became concerned that young people were using the convention of a woman's marrying her abductor or rapist to elope, to avoid obtaining parental permission to marry. By 1382, the Statute of Rapes—brought about primarily by a high-profile case of Sir Thomas West and the abduction and marriage of his daughter, Eleanor, in 1380—made two significant changes to the statute: first, it made the woman culpable in her own rape if she should consent after the fact; and, second, it specified that the woman be disinherited and forfeit her dowry.[7] The definition of rape had changed from a physical felony against the body of a woman to a trespass and property crime against a family.

Rape in "The Wife of Bath's Tale"

It is in this context that Chaucer rewrote a traditional folk tale. In the traditional tale—which we have in at least two other versions, Gower's "Tale of Florent" and the anonymous "Wedding of Dame Ragnell"—the story begins with a young, high-status knight who kills the wrong person in a fair fight. The knight is honourable, and, significantly, is named—Florent, nephew to the emperor in Gower's version, and Gawain, nephew to King Arthur in the "Wedding of Dame Ragnell." The quest the knight goes on, to discover what women want, is an "impossible task" set to avoid the tricky situation of punishing someone of such a high status (he agrees that if he fails in the task, he loses his head). Women, in these stories, are figured as the unknowable Other, and thus trying to find out what they want is *supposed* to be unanswerable from the start. The ugly old lady gives the knight the condition of her answering the question—that he marry her—*before* providing him with the correct answer; and then once they are married and in bed together, she suddenly becomes beautiful, and gives him a fairy-tale choice of having her beautiful by day and ugly by night, or ugly by day and beautiful by night.

Chaucer changed the traditional story in several key details—details especially significant in the heated context in the 1380s of a debate about rape, women's choice, and women's sovereignty. Rather than being named and a close relation to the ruler, his knight is nameless and is simply a member of Arthur's court. Rather than making the quest a way to get the knight killed, the queen and her ladies give the quest as a way to *save* the knight from capital punishment. The quest is a real quest, not an "impossible task," and they really think he might be able to figure out "what women want." Chaucer's knight gives a "rash promise" to the old woman—I will do whatever you want, if you give me the answer, he tells her—rather than finding out beforehand that the price of her answer is marriage; and this sets up his own "rape" when he finds out that the fulfillment of his promise involves marrying and thus having sex with her against his will. Chaucer's old lady then proceeds to give a three-page lecture on "gentilesse," "gentility" or true nobility. Chaucer's old woman does not change into a beautiful woman before giving the knight the beautiful-or-ugly choice, so he has to take it on trust that she can indeed change into a beautiful woman. And the choice she gives him is very different—rather than beautiful by night or by day, she gives him the classic anti-feminist choice, one that anti-feminist literature claimed every man faced: do you want a woman who is beautiful and unfaithful, or ugly and faithful?

But Chaucer's most significant change is in the initiating incident: Chaucer is the only writer to have the tale start with a rape.

And Chaucer makes it very clear that this is a rape in our meaning of the word—violent forced sex—rather than elopement or seduction or abduction or anything else *raptus* could signify at the end of the fourteenth century. We are told,

> And so bifel that this kyng Arthour
> Hadde in his hous a lusty bacheler,
> That on a day cam ridynge fro ryver,
> And happed that, allone as he was born,
> He saugh a mayde walkynge hym biforn,
> Of which mayde anon, maugree hir heed,
> By verray force, he rafte hire maydenhed. (III.882–888)[8]

> [And it happened that this King Arthur
> Had in his house a lively young man
> Who one day went riding along the river
> And it happened that, alone as when he was born,
> He saw a maiden walking before him,
> Of which maiden then, despite anything she could do,
> By force, he took her maidenhead.]

That this is rape in our meaning of the word is unequivocal: Chaucer makes it clear that her maidenhead is "rafte" "by force" against her wishes ("maugree hir heed"). So the students are surprised when it is the *women* of Arthur's court who argue against the death sentence with which King Arthur "dampned" the knight, and even more surprised when he takes on the "heroic" role of going on a quest, succeeding at the quest, and being rewarded at the end after all. I find, whenever I teach this tale, that the students have a range of responses to these surprises—responses that are themselves similar to the varying interpretations provided by Chaucerian scholars. As I realized in that moment in February 2015, those responses are also freakily similar to the responses to the Dal Dentistry scandal.

Change Is Not Possible

The first group of responses fall into the "change is not possible" category. No one who could hold those attitudes, no one who could possibly think those jokes were funny, no one who could rape a woman, can ever fundamentally change. A significant portion of every class, along with many critics, believes that a rapist cannot possibly reform, and therefore the knight may have "figured out the correct response" by the end of the tale, but that he has not really changed. Elaine Tuttle Hansen writes: "The rapist not only saves his life but is also rewarded by the promise of that impossible being, an unfailingly beautiful, faithful and obedient wife."[9] Laurie Finke focuses on the legal aspect of the tale: "The court of law is replaced by a court of ladies and the violence of the state-sanctioned criminal punishment by the rituals of the game. The brutality of rape vanishes with hardly a trace."[10] Susanne Sara Thomas thinks that in light of the knight's "rather impressive and prolonged desire to remain ignorant of the meaning of his quest...he doesn't want to know what women want," and, because "the knight's resistance to the idea of female sovereignty is so pro-nounced and overdetermined," she calls his "apparent" learning by the end of the tale "too improbable to be believed."[11] For this group, no change or learning is possible for someone who could commit such a heinous crime, or hold such reprehensible attitudes in the first place.

It was the same with the dentistry scandal. A petition on change.org, calling for Dalhousie's administration to expel the students involved, said, "Not one individual, regardless of sex, age or gender, that participates in a group that condones violence toward women, including rape, the drugging of females and other misogynistic attitudes, should ever be placed in a position of trust...Not one person who believes the drugging of an individual as a way to have non-consensual sex is funny or a joke should ever have access to sedatives."[12] That petition amassed over a thousand signatures in an afternoon, forty thousand within a week, and fifty thousand by the time of my Chaucer lesson. A #dalhateswomen hashtag on Twitter received more than sixty thousand retweets. By the "no-change-is-possible" group, "restorative justice" is seen as a farce. Rebecca Kohler in the *Metro* newspaper wrote, "The current plan of action at Dalhousie is to resolve the situation through restorative justice, meaning everyone talks it out and then awkwardly hugs or something. But imagine being one of the women mentioned in the posts and having to sit across from one of the 'gentlemen' as he apologized to you...would you really believe that a man [who suggests such misogynist things] is going to apologize and mean it?"[13]

Jude Ashburn, a coordinator at Halifax's South House Sexual & Gender Resource Centre, said she believes the restorative justice process "has always been [only] about restoring Dalhousie's reputation."[14] And the provincial licensing bodies of dentists in Ontario and Alberta demanded the names of the thirteen men, regardless of whether they underwent the restorative justice process or not.

Punishment Should Send a Strong Message

The second group of responses admits the possibility of change and learning but still thinks the Dentistry men and the knight should have been punished. Critics and students both have trouble with the concept of the "rewarded rapist," whatever learning he might have undergone in the meantime. In other words, they acknowledge some learning on the part of the knight but think he still should have been "punished." Corinne Saunders admits the knight has learned something but objects to the larger structures of the tale: "the ending and final transformation here must remain disturbing: underlying the allure of the romance narrative is the hard fact of the rapist's gaining of a young, beautiful and apparently noble wife...While such a reading is attractive in offering a positive interpretation of the final transformation, it ignores the problematic role of the knight as rewarded rapist."[15] Similarly, Amy Vines complains, "what has continued to trouble critics about the end of this *Tale* is the fact that, regardless of the knight's intervening quest to discover women's desires and his eventual acceptance (sincere or otherwise) of the hag's *maisterye*, he is still a rapist who is not punished, but is ultimately rewarded for his crime."[16]

At Dal, there were calls to "send a strong message against rape culture" and to expel the students, whether or not they went through the restorative justice process. The hacker collective Anonymous threatened to release the thirteen men's names if they weren't expelled. A hashtag, "expel misogyny," started on Twitter. Protesters rallied in front of the Dentistry building with signs such as "Expel Rape Culture" and "Dalhousie Hates Women." There was a pervasive feeling that the Dal men "got off light" and that they were being protected by Dalhousie University. Dal was criticized on Twitter for approaching misogyny as a "teachable moment" rather than a pervasive problem. This group of responses wants to send a message that such behaviour and attitudes will not be tolerated, and believes that, even *if* the knight or the Dal Dentistry men learned something in the process, sending a clear message requires a clear, unequivocal, and traditional—meaning punitive—punishment.

Change Heads Rather Than Remove Them

The third group, in both cases, believes that changing society is more important than punishment or revenge, and that the only way to change society as a whole is by changing one person at a time. Elizabeth Biebel makes the point that punishment alone will not change society: "While employing capital punishment would certainly ensure that the rapist knight would never become a repeat offender, we should ask how his death might act as a preventative strike against rape. Obviously, the threat of death did not deter the knight from committing rape [in the first place]."[17] Jill Mann is one of the strongest supporters of the ending of the tale, saying, "The punishment [the queen] devises is not designed to 'let him off lightly,' but to act as an educative process which will eradicate the male mentality that produced the crime;...It is a punishment that fits the knight's crime, since the question of what women desire is presumably something that never enters a rapist's head."[18] Thomas Van likewise says, "the women [of the court] see an ironic connection between an unthinking act and an unthinking punishment for it, and also the waste in separating an act from its causes and underlying assumptions, or from other similar acts. Mechanical retribution, although probably cathartic, would also end any discussion about why that knight raped that woman. The queen and her company realize too well what the consequences of treating rape as an isolated act have been. They want to change the insides of a head the law proposes simply to remove."[19] Numerous other critics could be quoted, but what all of these critics have in common is the beliefs that, first, people can change, and second, that the knight has indeed changed by the end of the tale.

The restorative justice process in the Dal Dentistry scandal generated a similar group of responses. The final report on the restorative justice process at Dalhousie was released in May 2015, and contained this statement from the women involved:

> Restorative justice provided us with a different sort of justice than the punitive type most of the loudest public voices seemed to want. We...were not looking to have our classmates expelled as 13 angry men who understood no more than they did the day the posts were uncovered. Nor did we want simply to forgive and forget. Rather, we were looking for a resolution that would allow us to graduate alongside men who understood the harms they caused, owned these harms, and would carry with them a responsibility and obligation to do better...Contrary to the more traditional form of justice, we were looking for positive changes rather than punishments.[20]

A *Globe and Mail* editorial, one of the few media outlets that came out on the side of Richard Florizone, Dalhousie's president, ventured the opinion that "justice will be best served if anyone found wanting is required to sit uncomfortably across a table from his victims and learn first-hand why his comments were damaging...If that happens, Dr. Florizone will have taken an ugly moment and turned it into a teachable one. We call that education."[21]

So that irruptive event, that dissonant moment in *The Canterbury Tales* class, let me realize how similar the responses to the two cases were, but also how much depended on the assumptions and values already held by the people responding. If a person believes that someone who would rape a woman, or someone who would post jokes about rape on Facebook, is never really going to change, then he or she probably disagrees with both Queen Guenivere and Richard Florizone and thinks that the offenders should be prosecuted to the full extent of the law—that is, killed or expelled—so they never have a chance to commit the crime again. If one believes people only stop being misogynists because of a fear of punishment, and that institutions can only send a clear message against "rape culture" by being seen to punish rapists and misogynists harshly, then one will fall into the second group: regardless of whether the offender has learned or changed, and even if he has, he still should have been punished. If, on the other hand, a student or citizen believes that people and society *can* change and should be given the chance to do so, then that student or citizen will probably approve of an approach—be it a quest or, the more modern version, a restorative justice process—that gives misogynists the opportunity to learn how women really feel.

In the weeks after that moment in class, we realized that the Dal Dentistry scandal and "The Wife of Bath's Tale" are alike in another way too. In both cases the injured women seem to disappear—for example, when Dal delayed announcing the suspension of the male students until after Christmas, it did so because the administration had credible reports that some of the *men* were close to self-harm, but it apparently neglected to consider the feelings of the women, who would have spent the break wondering if they would have to sit next to one of the men in class the following term. Dal's Student Union, especially, kept asking why we were not hearing from the women involved. The raped maiden, similarly, simply disappears from "The Wife of Bath's Tale" and is never heard from again. We never find out if she recovers, marries, or is cast out of her family or community. Indeed, my comparison of the knight's quest to the restorative justice process is lacking one crucial step that usually takes place in restorative justice. In restorative justice, the goal is for the offenders to truly learn what their victims went through, and to internalize that learning so that they never do something similar again—and I truly think that is what the knight's quest in "The Wife of Bath's Tale" was meant to do, and why I think it is an apt comparison. But a key component of restorative justice is talking to the victims, and, more importantly, listening to them. The knight in the story, apparently, talks to every woman in the kingdom—*except* the raped maiden. She simply disappears.

But my students always note that times have changed since the Middle Ages. We have made "progress" in terms of gender equality and reducing (if not eliminating) misogyny since medieval times (haven't we?). The difference between medieval times and now is that, whereas we do not know whether anyone in the Middle Ages commented on the disappearance of the maiden, almost everyone today notices—nearly every single critic comments on her disappearance from the story. Likewise, condemnation of the omission of the Dal women's voices was pervasive, until the women *themselves* released a statement asking people (especially the Student Union) to stop speaking for them, saying,

> Many people (some with good intentions) have spoken about us and in the process often attempted to speak *for* us...Our perspective and decision to proceed through this process has often not been honoured or trusted but dismissed or criticized based on the decisions or perspectives of others. We are strong, well-educated professional women with words of our own to explain what we are going through and how we want to proceed.[22]

That is, even though the women themselves felt they were being heard, the society around them was insistent that their voices be heard.

But February 2015 was *before* the Backhouse report, charged with investigating Dal's handling of the incident, was released. Before we realized that Dal, too, had a maiden who was silenced, shunned, and who disappeared completely from the official story—to the point where most people did not even know of her existence. She does not appear in the report released by the participants in the restorative justice process. According to the Backhouse report, Dalhousie University's administration knew about the Facebook group a full week before the media got a hold of the story, because a woman it calls "Student A" took a screenshot of some of the Facebook posts and complained to the administration. Student A reports that she felt her concerns and needs continually went unmet and were ignored by the administration. She wanted to make a formal complaint and felt pressured to opt for an "informal process." The Backhouse report reads,

> Over the weekend, Student A's parents contacted the President of the University, the Dean of Dentistry, and other University officials. They were not satisfied with Dentistry's offer to isolate her from her classmates. They saw this as penalizing her while the abusers

maintained their normal routine. Instead the abusers should be the ones to be moved.[23]

Over the following weeks, as the story broke in the media, Student A felt increasingly shunned and isolated by her classmates. She was writing her exams in a separate room, and this was what the report calls "a dead giveaway" to her classmates that she had sent the Facebook posts to the university administration. The report goes on to say that, after Christmas, "The anger initially focused on the Facebook group seemed to have spread to [Student A] and to [the male whistleblower]. Both of them began to feel like the new scapegoats of the crisis." After the restorative justice report was released, Student A "protested that the report did not include her story" and that it demonstrated no respect for her or her opinions, or the decision she made not to participate in restorative justice. In the end, the Backhouse report states, "Student A...believed that she had been unfairly maligned for reporting the harassment to the University, falsely accused of having leaked documents to the CBC, ostracized by her peers, and denied her right to pursue her education in an atmosphere free from intimidation." She graduated separately from the rest of the class.

She, too, disappeared from the story. The following year, when I taught *The Canterbury Tales* again, my students could no longer console themselves with the thought of how far our society had come since the Middle Ages. Indeed, I made a point of noting that society in the Middle Ages—at least as represented in "The Wife of Bath's Tale"—treated women *better* than society does today. Chaucer explicitly says that the knight and the maiden were all alone. And they did not have rape kits in those days. The maiden apparently does not do any of the things that were required by the pre-1275 law—raising the hue and cry, displaying her torn clothing and defensive wounds. So, at court, it is just the maiden's word against the knight's.

Yet her version is *never* doubted, and a supposedly honourable, high-class knight is condemned to lose his head because of it. Indeed, many critics have speculated that the maiden herself must have been very high class or well connected for the court to believe her unquestioningly.[24] Chaucer, significantly, gives us no information as to her status.

The Violence of Teaching

In every class, every year, there will always be people—women, mostly—who have been raped. Or assaulted. Or abused. Some of them may even have taken their rapists or abusers to court. In the spring of 2015, two or three months after I taught the class on "The Wife of Bath's Tale," I was in court myself, watching a friend testify against her partner, who had assaulted and abused her. She had more evidence than the maiden in the story did—she had kept a journal of escalating incidents, and she had a list of friends she had talked to after the incidents. Yet *she* was treated like the criminal, doubted, tricked by the lawyer. After she was sworn in, she had to sit in the witness box for at least twenty minutes, in full view of her abuser, while his lawyer went back to his office to get the police report he had supposedly "forgotten." *Her* background was brought up; *her* text messages were analyzed, *her* emails were introduced as evidence. She was asked where she had slept the night of the assault, and why she waited until the next day to report it. Her accused abuser was never required to testify, and details of *his* past, and previous assaults on her, including one that landed her in the hospital, were considered inadmissible and irrelevant. In the end, he was let off scot-free—without even a quest to find out "what women want." Most students do not like to admit our society is *less* progressive than the Middle Ages. But if Chaucer was able to have *even just imagined* a case where a woman accusing a man of rape *would not have been doubted for an instant*—most students are forced to admit they could not imagine a similar case happening today.

I am sure that in every class there are individuals who have had similar experiences, or who did not take their attackers to court because they knew they would not be believed. This is where the violent aspect of "eventual pedagogy" inevitably intrudes. When I taught "The Wife of Bath's Tale" a year later, I could tell just by looking around the classroom, at the way they were sitting, that two of the women had almost certainly been raped or abused at some point. Significantly, they took no part in the discussion that day. And I did not know how to deal with that, how to balance my concern for their well-being with my need to leave space open for (possibly violent) evental irruptions.

Another problem with "evental pedagogy" affects the way I will teach "The Wife of Bath's Tale" in the future: the impossible singularity of that particular event, that particular moment. I could try to recreate the moment. I once had a professor for first-year English who was teaching Tennyson's "Lady of Shalott," who ran out of room on the chalkboard so started on impulse to write on the wall (it was chalk and brick back then, not whiteboard markers and paint!). He then brilliantly tied his act in with the theme of the poem, the theme of artists going beyond boundaries and breaking rules. I had the same professor two years later for a Victorian literature class, and, supposedly, accidentally, *he did exactly the same thing again* when teaching the same poem. Probably, the first time it happened it had been an actual accident, an "event," but it worked so well that in later years he decided to recreate it. I will not be able to do that. Perhaps other scandals will arise, but I will never again be teaching that tale in exactly the same context. The best I will be able to do is tell my story of that moment when I said, "Who here objects that the knight goes on to a successful career in dentistry?" And leave space open in the rest of my teaching for similar events, similar irruptions of insight and coincidence.

NOTES

1. "Dalhousie University Probes Misogynistic Student 'Gentlemen's Club,'" *CBC News*, December 15, 2014, http://www.cbc.ca/news/canada/nova-scotia/dalhousie-university-probes-misogynistic-student-gentlemen-s-club-1.2873918.

2. "Restorative justice," as opposed to "retributive justice," views crime as a violation of interpersonal and community relationships, rather than an offense against a government or state. Its focus is on the accused taking responsibility for his or her wrongdoing, rather than on inflicting punishment. Influenced by the beliefs and practices of Indigenous groups such as the Maori of New Zealand and the First Nations peoples of North America, as well as by the beliefs of faith communities such as the Mennonites and Amish, restorative justice has expanded in popularity over the past two decades. A groundbreaking work was Howard Zehr's 1990 book, *Changing Lenses: A New Focus for Crime and Justice* (Waterloo, ON: Herald Press, 1990). More resources exist than can easily be cited, but a good start is the Centre for Justice and Reconciliation (restorativejustice.org). For the report of the restorative justice process, see Jennifer J. Llewellyn, Jacob MacIsaac, and Melissa MacKay, *Report from the Restorative Justice Process at the Dalhousie University Faculty of Dentistry*, May 2015, https://www.dal.ca/content/dam/dalhousie/pdf/cultureofrespect/RJ2015-Report.pdf. For restorative justice in Nova Scotia, see the Nova Scotia Restorative Justice Community University Research Alliance (http://www.nsrj-cura.ca/) and the Government of Nova Scotia's Restorative Justice site (http://novascotia.ca/just/RJ/program.asp).

3. "Whatever kind of action relating to my rape or any other matter or cause" (translation mine).

4. Christopher Cannon, "*Raptus* in the Chaumpaigne Release and a Newly Discovered Document Concerning the Life of Geoffrey Chaucer," *Speculum* 68 (1993).

5. J.B. Post, "Sir Thomas West and the Statute of Rapes, 1382," *Historical Research* 53.127 (1980), 24.

6. Post, 24.

7. Post, "Sir Thomas West," 24–30; Suzanne Edwards, "The Rhetoric of Rape and the Politics of Gender in the Wife of Bath's Tale and the 1382 Statute of Rapes," *Exemplaria* 23.1 (2011), 10.

8. All quotations from *The Canterbury Tales* will be taken from the *Riverside Chaucer* and cited by fragment and line number. Geoffrey Chaucer, *The Riverside Chaucer*, 3rd ed., ed. Larry Benson et al. (Boston: Houghton-Mifflin, 1987); translations from Middle English are mine.

9. Elaine Tuttle Hansen, *Chaucer and the Fictions of Gender* (Berkeley: University of California Press, 1992), 33.

10. Laurie Finke, "'All Is for to Selle': Breeding Capital in the Wife of Bath's Prologue and Tale," in *Geoffrey Chaucer: The Wife of Bath*, ed. Peter Beidler (Boston: St. Martin's, 1996), 173.

11. Suzanne Sara Thomas, "The Problem of Defining *Sovereynetee* in the *Wife of Bath's Tale*," *The Chaucer Review* 41.1 (2006), 87.

12. Meghan B, "Petitioning Dalhousie University President Dr. Richard Florizone: Expel the Students Who Were Members and/or Participated in the Facebook Group Called 'Class of DDS 2015 Gentlemen,'" https://www.change.org/.

13. Rebecca Kohler, "Dalhousie Dentistry Scandal: Tasteless Joke or Harmful Threats?" *Metro Halifax*, January 9, 2015, https://www.pressreader.com/canada/starmetro-halifax/20150109/281788512437027.

14. John Last, "Restorative Justice Process Flawed, Say Victims of Dalhousie Dentistry Scandal," *The Fulcrum*, March 19, 2015, https://thefulcrum.ca/news/restorative-justice-process-flawed-say-victims-of-dalhousie-dentistry-scandal/.

15. Corinne Saunders, *Rape and Ravishment in the Literature of Medieval England* (Cambridge: D.S. Brewer, 2001), 305–6.

16. Amy Vines, "Invisible Woman: Rape as a Chivalric Necessity in Medieval Romance," in *Sexual Culture in the Literature of Medieval Britain,* ed. Amanda Hopkins et al. (Cambridge: D.S. Brewer, 2014), 167.

17. Elizabeth Biebel, "A Wife, a Batterer, a Rapist: Representations of 'Masculinity' in the Wife of Bath's Prologue and Tale," in *Masculinities in Chaucer*, ed. Peter Beidler (Cambridge: D.S. Brewer, 1998), 64.

18. Jill Mann, *Feminizing Chaucer* (Cambridge: Boydell & Brewer, 2002), 71.

19. Thomas Van, "False Texts and Disappearing Women in the 'Wife of Bath's Prologue and Tale,'" *The Chaucer Review* 29.2 (1994), 185–86.

20. Llewellyn, MacIsaac, and MacKay, *Report from the Restorative Justice Process*.

21. Scott Munn, "Dalhousie's Handling of Facebook Scandal Is the Right Way to Go," *The Globe and Mail*, January 5, 2015, https://www.theglobeandmail.com/opinion/editorials/dalhousies-handling-of-facebook-scandal-is-the-right-way-to-go/article22301628/.

22. "An Open Statement from the Participants in Dalhousie's Restorative Justice Process to Address Harms Related to the Dalhousie Dentistry Student (DDS2015) Facebook Group Posts Issued March 1st, 2015," Process to Address Dentistry Facebook Comments, May 28, 2015, http://www.dal.ca/cultureofrespect/background/process.html.

23. Constance Backhouse, Donald McRae, and Nitya Iyer, *Report of the Task Force on Misogyny, Sexism and Homophobia in Dalhousie University Faculty of Dentistry*, June 26, 2015, https://cdn.dal.ca/content/dam/dalhousie/pdf/cultureofrespect/DalhousieDentistry-TaskForceReport-June2015.pdf.

24. For only one example, see Thomas, "The Problem of Defining *Sovereynetee*," 91.

WORKS CITED

B, Meghan. "Petitioning Dalhousie University President Dr. Richard Florizone: Expel the Students Who Were Members and/or Participated in the Facebook Group Called 'Class of DDS 2015 Gentlemen.'" https://www.change.org/.

Backhouse, Constance, Donald McRae, and Nitya Iyer. *Report of the Task Force on Misogyny, Sexism and Homophobia in Dalhousie University Faculty of Dentistry*. June 26, 2015. https://cdn.dal.ca/content/dam/dalhousie/pdf/cultureofrespect/ DalhousieDentistry-TaskForceReport-June2015.pdf.

Biebel, Elizabeth. "A Wife, a Batterer, a Rapist: Representations of 'Masculinity' in the Wife of Bath's Prologue and Tale." In *Masculinities in Chaucer*, edited by Peter Beidler, 63–75. Cambridge: D.S. Brewer, 1998.

Cannon, Christopher. "*Raptus* in the Chaumpaigne Release and a Newly Discovered Document Concerning the Life of Geoffrey Chaucer." *Speculum* 68 (1993): 74–94.

Centre for Justice and Reconciliation. 2017. http://restorativejustice.org.

Chaucer, Geoffrey. *The Riverside Chaucer*. 3rd ed. Edited by Larry Benson et al. Boston: Houghton-Mifflin, 1987.

"Dalhousie University Probes Misogynistic Student 'Gentlemen's Club.'" *CBC News*. December 15, 2014. http://www.cbc.ca/news/canada/nova-scotia/ dalhousie-university-probes-misogynistic-student-gentlemen-s-club-1.2873918.

Edwards, Suzanne. "The Rhetoric of Rape and the Politics of Gender in the Wife of Bath's Tale and the 1382 Statute of Rapes." *Exemplaria* 23.1 (2011): 3–26.

Finke, Laurie. "'All Is for to Selle': Breeding Capital in the Wife of Bath's Prologue and Tale." In *Geoffrey Chaucer: The Wife of Bath*, edited by Peter Beidler, 171–88. Boston: St. Martin's, 1996.

Government of Nova Scotia. "Restorative Justice." 2013. http://novascotia.ca/just/RJ/ program.asp.

Hansen, Elaine Tuttle. *Chaucer and the Fictions of Gender*. Berkeley: University California Press, 1992.

Kohler, Rebecca. "Dalhousie Dentistry Scandal: Tasteless Joke or Harmful Threats?" *Metro Halifax*, January 9, 2015. https://www.pressreader.com/canada/ starmetro-halifax/20150109/281788512437027.

Last, John. "Restorative Justice Process Flawed, Say Victims of Dalhousie Dentistry Scandal." *The Fulcrum*, March 19, 2015. https://thefulcrum.ca/news/ restorative-justice-process-flawed-say-victims-of-dalhousie-dentistry-scandal/.

Llewellyn, Jennifer J., Jacob MacIsaac, and Melissa MacKay. *Report from the Restorative Justice Process at the Dalhousie University Faculty of Dentistry*. May 2015. https://www.dal.ca/content/dam/dalhousie/pdf/cultureofrespect/RJ2015-Report.pdf.

Mann, Jill. *Feminizing Chaucer*. Cambridge: Boydell & Brewer, 2002.

Munn, Scott. "Dalhousie's Handling of Facebook Scandal Is the Right Way to Go." *The Globe and Mail*, January 5, 2015. https://www.theglobeandmail.com/opinion/editorials/ dalhousies-handling-of-facebook-scandal-is-the-right-way-to-go/article22301628/.

Nova Scotia Restorative Justice Community University Research Alliance.
    http://www.nsrj-cura.ca.

"An Open Statement from the Participants in Dalhousie's Restorative Justice Process to
    Address Harms Related to the Dalhousie Dentistry Student (DDS2015) Facebook
    Group Posts Issued March 1st, 2015." Process to Address Dentistry Facebook
    Comments. May 28, 2015. http://www.dal.ca/cultureofrespect/background/process.
    html.

Post, J.B. "Sir Thomas West and the Statute of Rapes, 1382." *Historical Research* 53.127
    (1980): 24–30.

Saunders, Corinne. *Rape and Ravishment in the Literature of Medieval England*. Cambridge:
    D.S. Brewer, 2001.

Thomas, Suzanne Sara. "The Problem of Defining *Sovereynetee* in the *Wife of Bath's Tale*."
    The Chaucer Review 41.1 (2006): 87–97.

Van, Thomas. "False Texts and Disappearing Women in the 'Wife of Bath's Prologue and
    Tale.'" *The Chaucer Review* 29.2 (1994): 179–93.

Vines, Amy. "Invisible Woman: Rape as a Chivalric Necessity in Medieval Romance."
    In *Sexual Culture in the Literature of Medieval Britain*, edited by Amanda Hopkins et al.,
    161–80. Cambridge: D.S. Brewer, 2014.

Zehr, Howard. *Changing Lenses: A New Focus for Crime and Justice*. Waterloo: Herald Press,
    1990.

The Practice Is
the Teacher

ELY SHIPLEY

> Creating a poem is more important
> than having written poems.
>
> —CA Conrad, "Poetry and Ritual"

> Practice and all is coming.
>
> —Sri K. Pattabhi Jois, "Practice and All Is Coming"

> There is an out-
> side of language that is not silence.
>
> —Donald Revell, "An Instrument Also"

DEAR READER, I WAS A GENDER NONCONFORMING KID. I got picked on a lot at school. Sometimes the most dangerous place for me was in a classroom. Some teachers didn't know what to do with me. Sometimes the only safe place for me was in a classroom. Some teachers knew not to try to do anything except let me be me. Not that I necessarily knew who I was. My best teachers fostered such unknowing of self ("*Je est un autre!*").[1] These teachers saved me. These teachers made me know I could save myself. These teachers made me feel that my supposed uncertainty, my supposed confusion about myself, about gender, about sexuality, was not an issue. In fact, these teachers made me trust that this was a blessing, a gift, a powerful way of not only being in the world but of seeing the world. And I knew all of this through intuition, through inference.

They spoke to me about difficult things, but this issue of identity they never needed to name. Somehow they knew that it was for me to discover and name on my own. They knew it was for me to author. They knew not to cause harm, that peculiar and particular kind of harm of forcing a role, a narrative, onto another. I was lucky. I am grateful.

The first person I ever came out to was my high school English teacher. My high school English teacher had run a creative writing club after school when I was in junior high. Junior high was the height of my torment. Every day at school I was asked, "Are you a boy or a girl?" Every day at home my parents asked, "Why are you so moody?" They demanded, "Stop slouching. Smile. Pull your hair out of your face so people can see what a pretty girl you are." But I was not a girl and I could not tell them how the kids treated me. I am certain they would have medicated me with antidepressants or hormones that did not agree with my gender presentation. They would have fed me poisons, innocently believing they were an antidote. There was no place that felt safe for me. There was no place I was not surveilled.

I made into matter what I could not safely embody, on paper in songs, poems, fragments of prose, and drawings. Through imagination and its expression, I reinforced neural pathways that made me matter.

Dear Reader, even now, with at least one of your senses, you touch my words. I make an echo of my body. I make another body. Here, I don't fear your gaze, your touch.

That creative writing club after school became a kind of home. I was shy. I didn't share much of what I wrote. It would take me another decade to even begin the journey of coming to terms with being who I am. Making poems taught me about myself.

In many ways, it's strange to me that I now spend my working life as a professor, albeit one who teaches writing, specifically poetry writing. On the one hand, I felt terrorized in school. On the other, I found a mirror there that made me feel a little less alone. Perhaps this is the least I can try to offer my students. Regardless of who they think they are, I ask them to position themselves in ways so that they might reflect, even enlarge, and experience, perhaps, something very beautiful. Or conversely, they might reflect and frame, in miniature, an experience that once terrified them, and maybe still does.

Dear Reader, I want to show you something about perspective. Eileen Myles said a few years ago at the Associated Writing Programs Conference that "teaching writing is teaching consciousness."[2] Allen Ginsberg once said in an interview, "The only thing that can save the world is the reclaiming of the awareness of the world. That's what poetry does."[3] Since junior high, my best teacher has been the practice of writing itself. No one can teach you this; they can encourage you to see for yourself.

One day in the spring of 2000, I was invited to audit a poetry workshop taught by Richard Garcia. We did a mysterious writing activity. There was constraint, but chance was also involved. I learned of a new form and a new poet, a very important one. Since then, I've used the exercise in many classes and at the Dissonant Methods workshop held at the Banff Centre the summer of 2016. There is a way in which writing together has a kind of power. The space becomes very quiet and vibrates. The concentration creates an incredible kind of static, especially if the prompt gets the mind to work in a different way than it might normally, even a different way than it might normally when it's trying to make a poem. The guidelines for the activity we did provide a degree of support, a stability to the uneasiness of trying out something new. But there is enough openness that allows each writer to channel whatever they have to offer. It becomes a process of turning inward, of presence, and of offering something up, of devoting one's self to the simple act of doing.

Dear Reader, the only way to simulate the experience of the exercise I shared at the workshop is to try it. Please humour me (and maybe yourself) and follow these instructions. Please resist the temptation to read ahead. The way the surprises unfold a particular way of seeing and experiencing is essential to this activity. It will take about twenty minutes to half an hour.

The first part of this exercise asks you to make a list of four objects you would find in nature and one that is human-made. For example: stone, grass, moon, leaf, clock.

Once you have your list of objects, make a line in the form of a sentence to address each object. Be imaginative. For example: "Grass, your hair grows longer than my sister's." Or, "Stone, why do you shut your eyes?" You will have one line for each object for a total of five lines.

The second part of the exercise asks you to think of someone you miss. This should be a person and it can be a loved one, a friend, a family member, living or deceased. Once you have your person in mind, write five lines in the form of sentences describing some of the particular and quirky, or unique, things about that individual. This is an opportunity to emphasize specificity. Avoid being too general. Each sentence should begin with a person's name or relation to the writer. In other words, they should be the subject of the sentence. For example, "My grandpa had three army tattoos: a black cat, the number thirteen, and a skull."

Once you have written all of these, you are going to pair the two parts of this exercise, alternating the first and second sets of descriptions to form couplets. For example:

Stone, why do you shut your eyes?
My grandpa had three army tattoos: the black cat, the number thirteen, and a skull.

Grass, your hair grows longer than my sister's.
My grandpa played himself at Chess, late into the night.

Pair up your lines, either by rewriting them or simply indicating which line goes with which by using numbers, letters, arrows, circles, or other notes.

What happened for you? Remember that this is a chance operation and an experiment. We just want to see what happens.

What are the effects of putting *seemingly* random descriptions together? Beyond discussing chance and juxtaposition, how does the use of personification, address, and a statement or a question about the object in one line work next to a line about the person who is missed? You might consider the limits of metaphor. If pushed far enough, it collapses. One thing is not another. Consider also the feeling of fact in the form of a statement or the implication of a question. Notice how the initial line in each couplet informs the next. It's likely that the first line sets a tone about the person who is missed.

Finally, look up Paul Celan's poem "Aspen Tree," which this prompt is modelled after, in order to read it in its entirety.[4] It's widely available online. Read the poem closely. Look up Celan's biography and read particularly about his mother. Consider how his couplets work together. What is the technique, beyond juxtaposition, in each couplet that tethers the lines? You might revise your poem to solidify any connections you may see in your exercise. Of course, you might mix and match or change your lines entirely.

NOTES

1. Arthur Rimbaud to Georges Izambard, May 13, 1871, *Lettres du Voyant*, https://www.scribd.com/document/157490650/Lettre-a-Georges-Izambard-du-13-mai-1871.

2. Eileen Myles (lecture, Associated Writing Programs Conference, Seattle, WA, 2014).

3. Allen Ginsberg, *Spontaneous Mind: Selected Interviews 1958–1996* (New York: Harper Collins, 2002), 173.

4. Paul Celan, "Aspen Tree," in *Poems of Paul Celan*, trans. Michael Hamburger (New York: Persea, 1995), 41.

WORKS CITED

Celan, Paul. "Aspen Tree." In *Poems of Paul Celan*, translated by Michael Hamburger, 41. New York: Persea, 1995.

Conrad, CA. "Poetry and Ritual." *Literary Hub*, February 5, 2016. http://lithub.com/poetry-ritual/.

Ginsberg, Allen. *Spontaneous Mind: Selected Interviews 1958–1996*. New York: Harper Collins, 2002.

Jois, Sri K. Pattabhi. "Practice and All Is Coming." *Yoga Journal*, June 22, 2009. https://www.yogajournal.com/yoga-101/practice-and-all-is-coming.

Myles, Eileen. Lecture presented at the Associated Writing Programs Conference, Seattle, WA, 2014.

Revell, Donald. "An Instrument Also." In *Beautiful Shirt*, 54–55. Hanover and London: Wesleyan University Press, 1994.

Rimbaud, Arthur. Arthur Rimbaud to Georges Izambard, May 13, 1871. *Lettres du Voyant*. https://www.scribd.com/document/157490650/Lettre-a-Georges-Izambard-du-13-mai-1871.

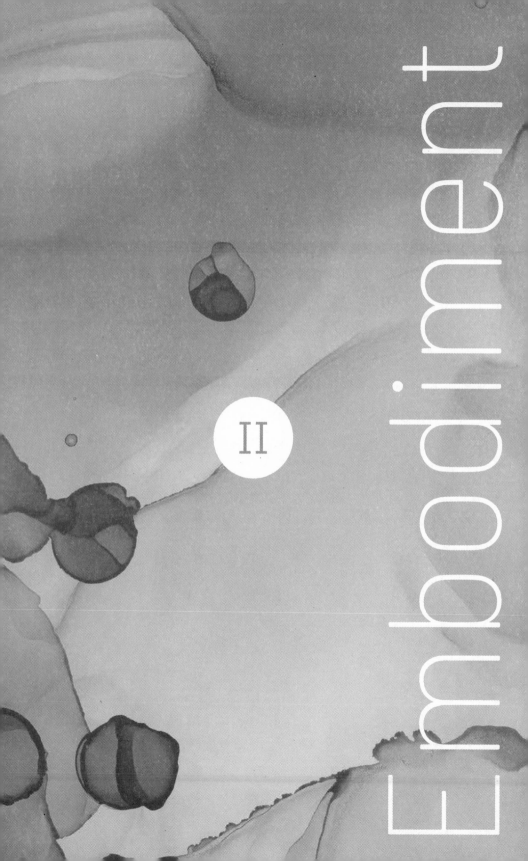

II

Embodiment

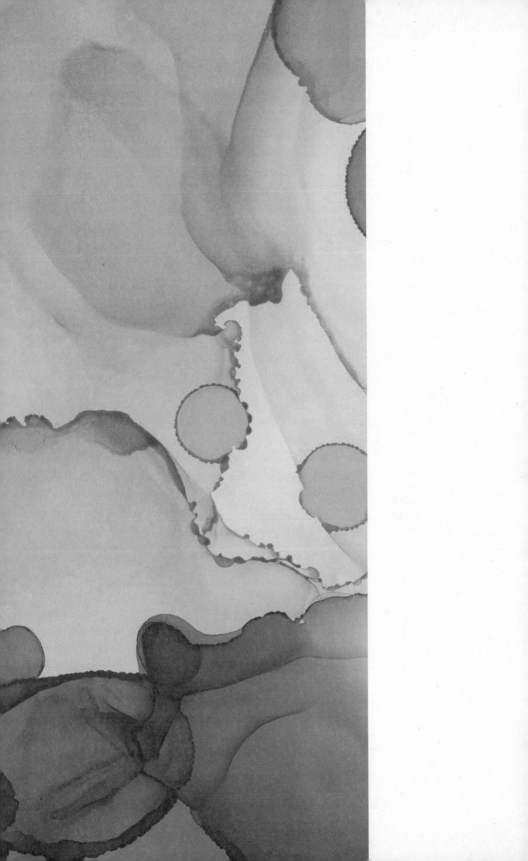

4

The Ecology of Attention

KATJA K. PETTINEN

> The word "learning" undoubtedly denotes change of some kind.
> To say what kind of change is a delicate matter.
>
> —Gregory Bateson, *Steps to an Ecology of Mind*

A Tomato Is Not a Vegetable but a Fruit (Unless It Is)

A common limitation in traditional accounts of education is the
overemphasis on memorization and other forms of standardization.
In his classic criticism of a system that aims to teach students the "facts,"
Paolo Freire referred to this as the "banking model of education."[1] In such
a model, learning is assumed to occur as a set of deposits that experts
install into the minds of novices, presumably sculpting the essence of
their character in controlled ways.

Such models of learning remain present in many science classrooms,
including social science, despite the extensive criticism brought forth over
the past several decades. One of the reasons for this persistence might be the
fact that this model of learning positions experts in a particularly *comfortable*
position: their authority is affirmed in the system every step of the way. As a
result, the experts can bestow the wisdom they have "acquired" through their
own learning upon the students, who can at best ask clarifying questions about
the content, yet are rarely encouraged to actually think critically about the material itself or about the nature of the very system in which they are positioned.
The word "tomato," as we are using it in this book (see the Introduction for more

about "tomatoes"), refers to the design choices deployed by teachers in the class-room, choices that reflect highly particular epistemological presumptions about teaching and learning. For example, using this analytic, the pedagogical tomato, "a tomato is not a vegetable but a fruit," might be evoked and come to operate as a form of final truth telling—promising that it will bring forth a robust and a clear change in the learners. (Learners will come to understand, by way of the expert's knowledge sharing, that tomatoes fall within the taxonomical category of "fruit," despite whatever commonsensical presumptions about "fruit" that students might unwittingly bring with them to the classroom).

However, when such a system of knowledge does not actually deliver the stability that it promises (warranting the premise that, for example, facts should remain as facts in the context of teaching and learning), one of the obvious side effects is a broader disenchantment toward the system itself, and in some cases, a full refusal.[2] In the context of scientific education, for example, we find a certain social erosion of the epistemological authority of science in the twenty-first century, such as vaccine refusals, as well as global warming and evolution deniers. Indeed, grand promises of education, includ-ing science, being able to deliver stable final truths about the world can only fail, given that the nature of our existence is dynamic, not stable and homeo-static. In other words, we are living systems existing within a multitude of co-evolutionary relations.[3]

In this chapter, I approach this classic challenge of learning, stability, and change through an embodied lens: I bring forth a contextualized case study of somatic learning, including a critique of the commonplace Cartesian model of embodied skill. As a whole, the "tomato" that is being evoked more fully in this chapter is comprised of two moves, rather than solely one. First, a tomato is not a vegetable but a fruit. In this first step, the scientific and biological truth about how tomatoes exist in the world contrasts with our pragmatic ways of interacting with tomatoes, and *this is a worthwhile point to recognize* in and of itself—it expands our knowledge and offers something important about the real, biological relations that exist in this world as a result of broader evolution-ary patterns. Yet, if we were to offer guests in our house yogurt for breakfast, we might add some fresh blueberries or other items commonly, *culturally*, *and socially* perceived as fruit, but we will not add tomato. To do so would be funda-mentally idiosyncratic and strange, and an appeal to a scientific "truth" would hardly make our guests any more comfortable, even if the guests in question were scientists themselves.

The second part of the pedagogical tomato that this chapter evokes concerns the limitations of the expert-driven approach to teaching and learning that I describe above. It involves a parenthetical addition: the tomato is not a vegetable but a fruit (unless it is). This addition, "unless it is," is premised upon the fact that, while a biological and scientific taxonomy of a tomato might well contrast with the pragmatic domain, there are no absolute, context-free taxonomies. In other words, we can recognize as learners something that at first glance might seem contradictory: namely, that in a biology course the real answer to how tomatoes exist in the world is to classify them as fruit and not as vegetable, but that such truths cannot, and need not, reach into all domains of life. If we are to engage in a process of learning, we will submit ourselves to a certain authority of previous bodies of knowledge that are relevant in a given context *while also remembering* the most basic fact about contexts, namely that they change and vary. As such, we can recognize that there are knowledges that tell us something about the world but that not everything is reducible to scientific authority, even when such knowledge remains relatively stable. Because contexts matter for all forms of knowledge, the desire for omnipotent and absolute knowledge is a poor Enlightenment hangover laden with colonialist leanings, some of which Namrata Mitra examines in her chapter of this book. The "tomato" in this chapter reflects a dissonant method of teaching in that it foregrounds the importance of scientific facts (like the correct taxonomical understanding of tomatoes as fruit), while also contextualizing and even querying such facts in light of pragmatic practices (like the dietary and cultural patterns that preclude tomatoes from joining strawberries or melons in a fruit salad).

(Dis)Embodied Learning

One of the central characteristics of post-secondary learning is that it does not place focus upon doing much at all with and through our bodies. Rather than being a path to learning, bodies are treated as potential sources for diagnosis. If a learner is placing extensive focus upon their own body over the classroom itself, they will potentially be diagnosed as having a disorder of some kind with their attention span. Within the actual pragmatics of social life, attention spans operate within a complex and messy ecology; students come to the classroom with previous experiences, many of which can re-sort the priorities of their attention from day to day. Of course, economies of attention also exist, given that capitalist parameters reach into most corners of the university, impacting the attentional capacities of both teachers and students alike. While I recognize the fact that economies of capitalism fundamentally structure the classroom, I prefer to think about attention more ecologically, highlighting the ways in which attention and perception exist within a multitude of relations, many of which reach far beyond the human form (say, into the various biota within and across our bodies).

A common feature of the Scholarship of Teaching and Learning (SoTL) is to recognize that an interdisciplinary endeavour requires shifting the contexts of learning[4]—otherwise one's account of teaching and learning would be far too narrow, even idiosyncratic, to work as an overall account of the varying processes involved. In part due to a gap in SoTL scholarship when it comes to somatic learning, I address the overall question of embodiment in this chapter, thus allowing SoTL scholars to think about learning in a more holistic way. Specifically, I do this through an ethnographically grounded case study on the processes of teaching and learning in the context of a Japanese martial art being studied in English-speaking North America.

Learning to Do Things with the Body

According to one all-too-common representation of learning, the acquisition of new skills occurs through one quality in particular: repetition. In such representations, for example, a student might perform a distinct set of movements over and over in order to achieve an ability to execute those movements with such efficiency that they achieve a kind of "automated" or even "second nature." Consider how the 1980s movie, *The Karate Kid*, reflects this kind of stereotypical representation of bodily skills in its depiction of Asian martial arts. In the movie, a novice student of karate learns to hone his ability to defend against kicks and strikes through a circular hand block that he practises by waxing cars, repeating the mantra "wax on, wax off." The student learns another method of blocking by painting a wooden fence, in this case using his hand vertically up and down. In the movie, the method of learning bodily skills is represented as a process that is not dependent upon context: the process can be isolated away from the space or relations in which it is utilized without compromising its efficacy for skill acquisition. Moreover, this learning takes place without any intention on the part of the student. The learner has no awareness of the fact that he is learning skilled movement patterns, skills he will later utilize in order to defend himself. He acquires his skills solely through so-called muscle memory, with attention but with no intention. The body, according to this representation, is an entity that can stand distinctly apart from the mind, the self, and its embodied, contextual relations.

In this chapter, I suggest this model of learning is not simply a popular culture oddity but one that reflects deeply held Western assumptions about the nature of learning itself. While *The Karate Kid* does not aim to engage with the nuances of human cognition or neurology, the overall representation of skill in the film aligns closely with two common North American conceptions of cognitive and bodily learning processes:

1. Certain kinds of movement patterns are distinct abilities, skills that an individual achieves over time through repetitive training and practice.

2. These distinct abilities reside solely in the physicality or "muscle memory" of the individual, and therefore they can be acquired, out of context, and then performed on command.

Such models leave out any room for thinking about the *emergent nature* of learning, or learning as a nonlinear and nonpredictable process,[5] one that is as much about the absence, rather than the presence, of things. Further, learning as an emergent process also echoes the dynamic nature of living systems themselves.

I examine martial arts learning in this chapter for two main reasons. First, it can be useful to look at an entirely other context than the classroom as a way to prompt new insights or questions about teaching and learning: a martial arts dojo (school) provides an especially instructive context along these lines. There are shared assumptions between stereotypical representations of martial arts (as found in *The Karate Kid*, for example) and conventional accounts of learning in the university; these assumptions are often so naturalized within classrooms that they are difficult to notice or scrutinize, especially in terms of mind/body connections. I bring martial arts into the conversation in order to render these presumptions more available for scrutiny.

Second, there are *other*, more dissonant approaches to learning at play within martial arts, approaches that have tremendous promise for rethinking classroom methods. Relying in part upon my ethnographic analysis of a Japanese martial art, taijutsu, in what follows, I describe key aspects of these alternative approaches to learning. What's central to my argument is the interdependence of ontology with epistemology. Put differently, while it is clear that years or decades of martial arts practice shape the mind/body of each practitioner, this shaping takes place through *epistemological* as well as *somatic* practices. There is an intelligence to bodily movements, on this account, an intelligence that is as relevant to classroom contexts as it is to martial arts practice.

Models of Learning at the Intersections
of Epistemology and Ontology

English-speaking North Americans often invoke the phrase, "putting in your ten thousand hours," as a way to explain the process of skill acquisition.[6] In this paradigm, skill is assessed in terms of the efficiency of movements (and movements predominantly centre on the upper body).[7] If one *puts in* one's ten thousand hours, then repetition secures the promise of successfully acquiring a particular skill. Simply put in your ten thousand hours and you'll become an expert!

North American taijutsu practitioners tend to invoke this concept of a "motor skill" when they describe their own learning experiences. (The backdrop here is key: these are North Americans who seek to learn a Japanese martial art but, at least initially, import their own North American paradigms of learning in order to do so). Most commonly, this concept of "skill" refers to the kind of manipulation one is able to achieve through the movement of one's hands: for example, in the execution of a wrist lock. In this model, learning presumably occurs as a result of accumulation. Skill emerges through an increase of internalized representations that become reified through repeated movements over time ("ten thousand hours"). This account of internalization, common in the so-called second-wave cognitive science,[8] is part of the same broader paradigm that regards student memorization of facts in classrooms as a meaningful way of becoming an educated citizen. Such notions of internalized mental representations—whether a set of memorized facts or "automated" movement patterns that a student learns though imitation—have in part been historically conditioned by the rise of computerized technologies, which indeed can be programmed through coding. Yet the commonly forgotten, key aspect of such technologies is the fact that they are not organic, living systems.

The emphasis on repetition syncs with a broader understanding of the body (and the mind) as *mechanical*. More than solely a model of learning, this paradigm reflects a broadly distributed set of discourses and practices that foreground the body as an entity that can be broken into parts and trained to perform on command. Ethnographically, one might hear key linguistic phrases such as "tuning up the machine," "getting the body running right," and "mind over matter"—phrases that are reflective of sports training more generally. These notions are highly culturally prevalent: they are most evident in the context of sports and the military but are also present in a number of approaches to medicine.[9] Along these lines, many North American dojos approach teaching the art through a linear and standardized curriculum. For example, instructors commonly assign particular textual programs to their students. Such programs often include "key terms" or "syllabi," listing movements that each student should be proficient in to advance through belt ranks.

But while North American students seek to affirm the acquisition of skills by pointing to repetition, Drew Leder explains that there is a paradox at play here. Within this paradigm, the learner's body is better described as a *disappearing body*, he explains, rather than a present and aware body. As a learner, I place my hope in the repetition of ten thousand hours, rather than on my own body: "I may be engaged in a fierce sport, muscles flexed and responsive to the slightest movements of my opponent. Yet it is precisely upon this opponent, this game, that my attention dwells, not on my own embodiment."[10] How fascinating that a body can "disappear" even in the context of practising a "fierce sport" like taijutsu!

Here is the crux of my argument. The tradition of taijutsu can certainly be considered a "fierce sport," of a kind along the lines Leder describes. However, this Japanese art aims to cultivate a distinctly different approach toward embodiment and learning than the paradigm of the disappearing body. Taijutsu is a noncompetitive martial art in which advanced skill centres on a *fusion* of doing with sensing; advanced skill involves a process of heightened perception in which the body itself comes to form a "thematic object of experience." In a central way this is the case precisely because the field of capacities that taijutsu aims to cultivate is broader than what any traditional sporting context utilizes; there are no rules in self-defense. Even further, an icy sidewalk does not have any intent to harm—yet slipping on ice is a very common way in which humans in northern locations injure themselves. Ice presents distinct harm and danger to us as bipedal primates, now consistently distracted by an ever-increasing set of portable technologies that beckon our attention elsewhere than on the movement of our bodies on a variable substrate.

The broader point here is that no matter what we choose to teach—in self-defense, in critical thinking, or in science—the actual fields of engagement for any learner are much broader than any given set of focus areas in our curricula are able to cover. At times this basic observation leads into questions of "applicability": Can the materials covered in our classes or seminars actually be applied to the real world? Many students have learned to ask, "Where can I actually use this?" Rather than foregrounding this form of thinking, much of it already too predetermined by the logics of capitalism and product development, in this chapter I suggest that a more productive framing deals with a meta-cognitive pattern, one that centres on learning to learn.

Studying Feeling in Movement

Translated into English, the term "taijutsu" evokes an "art of the body," a term that suggests an overall orientation toward using one's whole body in manipulating the balance of others. (This emphasis on the whole body contrasts with an approach that relies primarily on one's hands or arms for such manipulation). Historically, this art reflects the traditional Japanese fighting arts that emerged among the samurai, or the warrior class, of the early state formations starting in the eighth century.[11] Taijutsu draws from nine different martial lineages that are brought into cohesion by one single master teacher, or *soke*, Masaaki Hatsumi, born in Japan in 1931. Hatsumi began his study of the martial arts at an early age and, over the following decades, came to form his own synthesis of *budo*, or the martial way. He is the sole originator of the overall organization, or the interconnected web of training groups across the world that are generally referred to as Bujinkan, through which he transmits the art of taijutsu.

As a whole, taijutsu training emphasizes an attunement of the senses and of the perceptive system, thus focusing attention on more than what might, on the surface, appear to be the art's main feature: namely, the physicality of *doing*. Put simply, an advanced skill in taijutsu involves the ability to use perception, including one's own movement, as a vehicle for knowledge, as a means through which to understand the kinesthetic situation at hand. Because of this emphasis on using the body, including kinesthetic and proprioceptive sensation, as a means of interpreting dimensions of time and space, the practice cultivates what philosopher David Abram calls the "felt intelligence of our muscled flesh."[12] In other words, taijutsu demonstrates a perspective toward bodily knowledge in an analogous manner to the phenomenological method in continental philosophy that foregrounds "the body...[as] the primary instrument of all our knowing."[13]

One broader question that this ethnographic work on taijutsu skill raises is the overall ways in which we might shift the presence of the body within classrooms of higher education. Are there, for example, ways in which we might affirm and productively utilize, rather than readily diagnose, the kinds of affective states that both students and teachers inevitably bring with them to the classrooms? What might a phenomenologically attuned classroom look like? Specifically, what would a phenomenology informed through an analysis of *movement*—rather than through expecting the body to function as a perceptive system in stasis, as if part of still life painting—look like?

Truth and Authority

In many educational systems, rote memorization is utilized as an index of learning (such as in standardized testing) and presumably as a potential pathway to "knowledge." And, certainly, whether accessed through bodily (as "drills") or mind-centred pathways, memorization can provide a great degree of comfort for learners, at times even resembling addiction.[14] However, while both repetition and memorization can increase predictability in a closely defined field—a field that never changes—neither is a productive means for engaging or making sense of a dynamic world. This is a key emphasis of taijutsu training, for example, in contrast to a more classic sports training where drills and the idea of motor skills can remain at the centre because there is a ring, a sporting field, and pre-determined starting time. Because taijutsu aims to cultivate an overall means of protecting one's well-being, from whatever shape danger might take, including slipping on that icy sidewalk, the art cannot rely on predictable, context-free movements as a means of learning on a more general level. Indeed, many advanced practitioners of the art remind their students that no matter how long one trains, there can be no guarantees of keeping one's self from harm.

In a similar fashion, a more epistemically nuanced science education has to take into account the fact that science will never be completed, for one, given that the scientific method never proves anything—the null hypothesis can only be rejected in a "successful" experiment. Or, on another level, given that change is part of the world in which we live—think, for example, of climate change or epidemiology (in which the world is viewed as a complex and a dynamic system). As a result, a long-standing issue in science education is how to deal with the fact that the vast majority of things memorized from a textbook in a given decade will be revised, revisited, even flat out rejected in the coming decades.[15] Pluto was categorized as a planet until this accepted view became challenged and revised—and in that process, the old textbooks with their nuanced illustrations and logical explanations have become help-lessly out of date. Rather than pretending as if the facts do not change, science education, and education at large, including SoTL, must recognize and reflect on this fundamental feature of our socially most esteemed system of know-ledge, science: it cannot provide universal, absolute truths. Again, such an expectation was a poor result of the Enlightenment, *culturally particular*, and a strange expectation in the first place, in a similar fashion to the concept of objectivity.[16]

One particular aspect about learning and dynamism that is readily recognized in taijutsu is the fact the even the "master teacher" (*soke*) continues to change his approach to the art. In this embodied context, it is explicit that the advanced teachers are themselves continuing to learn and study movement. In a related fashion, previous SoTL scholars have noted that much of the actual processes involved in studying and comprehending a given system (be it aesthetic, biological, or social) are left out from the teaching process.[17] While no system of knowledge can articulate everything into language—some things will remain on a tacit level—what is clear in the context of taijutsu is that teachers will themselves keep changing and learning, that there is no absolute stability to expertise. I suggest that it is this fact of learning that higher education, including science education, might more readily recognize, shifting more attention to the inherently unsteady position of the expert, particularly across time—the recognition that no teacher, professor, or "esteemed scientist" has ended her own reassessment and re-evaluation of the system that she is herself examining. There is always more to discover in science, in movement, in life. Foregrounding this fact would indeed complicate the issue of social authority for education and for science, yet it would also make the relationships across epistemology (what is knowing?), ontology (overall domain of existence), and a given set of methods (always partial, not absolute) more honest. We get hints of such restructuring in the writings of physicist Marcelo Gleiser, who has recently cast science as an "island of knowledge," an articulation directly contrasting with the European Enlightenment-based desire to reach omnipotence (which feminist science and technology studies thinkers commonly refer to as weak objectivity).[18]

Another general issue at hand is that the sheer memorization of facts or of "drilling" one's body to execute a set of predetermined responses is not learning. This is the case because such procedures by themselves cannot provide actual skill sets for a living, ongoing, changing world—a dynamic world in which contexts for our knowledge will keep changing and new kinds of problems and questions will keep emerging. On another temporal level, even though there are general patterns that do reach across time in a relatively robust way (say, the scientific truth about a tomato being a fruit not a vegetable), such truths do not apply in all contexts of our lives. Even in the "here and now," we cannot simply swallow knowledge without reflecting on where and how it matters, recognizing that in some moments (offering your house guest yogurt for breakfast), the scientific truth does not matter because the pragmatic truth (tomatoes are culturally treated as a vegetable) is far more relevant.

Teaching a Living Art

Hatsumi evokes the concept of a living art, where even the fundamental techniques are executed with a differing emphasis from year to year, and especially decade to decade. As a whole, the art is a distinct synthesis of patterns emerging and diffusing, one where, in contrast to predetermined ways of executing particular movements, there is a great emphasis for each practitioner to be able to move in ways that best fit a given kinesthetic context. Of course, part of each kinesthetic context—the specific meeting of two bodies in time, space, and place—also includes the overall physiological makeup of each practitioner. As a result, practitioners need to develop a personal comportment in the art, instead of simply copying or imitating their instructors.

Because each basic movement, or technique, is always taught with a range of variations (such as being attacked while sitting down instead of standing up, or being attacked with a weapon), the practitioners study each movement in varying contexts, thus studying *relationships* more than any individual techniques. Moreover, a significant part of learning in taijutsu centres on having techniques, such as wrist and joint locks, done to your own body by more advanced practitioners. In this way, the bodily storytelling ripples out from Japan through the practitioners who travel there to learn from Hatsumi and from his Japanese senior students. A key element in this storytelling,[19] and the overall process of learning the art, is the experience of vulnerability that many of the techniques demonstrate when they are directly experienced through one's own senses.

In the course of such learning, practitioners are *not* thought of as coming to possess an ever-increasing set of skills, as conceptions of learning based on accumulation suggest. Rather, the longer-term goal of taijutsu practice is at times described as "becoming zero" or "empty." In his teaching, Hatsumi often tells people to "throw away their technique" in order to allow the art itself to come through. He therefore emphasizes that advanced skill in taijutsu is not about the possession of more and more techniques but rather about the ability to empty oneself of any such predetermined and reified patterns of movement. The expression of "becoming zero" stands in distinct tension with models of learning based on accumulation, which foreground closely defined contexts and high degrees of predictability for the form through which a somatic skill is expressed, thus prioritizing execution and performance over perception. In taijutsu practice, the ability to move and "do" things is, of course, also fundamental, but such ability is enabled through the movement of the feet, and through the perceptive system at large, instead of through the movement of hands and arms.

When we look more carefully at the details that allow advanced practitioners to execute a wrist lock efficiently each time, one key element is the ability to respond to variation *across* different body types and personalities, as well as across particularities of unique contexts (such as the kind of surface one is standing on: grass, gravel, or smooth floor). While on some level the attack might look "the same" each time, the advanced practitioner's sensorial ability to treat each attack as its own unique kinesthetic and temporal setting is one of the defining characteristics of advanced skill in taijutsu practice.[20]

Learning to Learn

By studying the nature of somatic learning within particular cultural contexts, we gain a rich perspective on the ways in which cultural processes are encoded in and through bodies in the scope of social life.[21] Overall, the ethnographic work on skill transmission and learning strongly supports the idea that somatic learning is neither linear nor accumulative in nature. The term "accumulative" suggests that learning takes place as a result of increased internalized representations; while this notion was prevalent in the second wave of cognitive studies, it is challenged by more recent work that highlights embodied and situated cognition.[22] Contemporary cognitive studies foreground how cognition is distributed not only throughout the body and the nervous system but also beyond the organism itself.[23]

In contrast to mechanical models, a number of recent studies on somatic skill and expertise demonstrate an inherent multimodality involved in learning and transmission. Ethnographic studies of skill development, for example, show that learners utilize varied routes, including imitation, observation, verbal explanation, the experience of pain and discomfort, visual diagrams, and other forms of modelling, in order to attain specific somatic codes deemed central to given somatic traditions. As a whole, such studies demonstrate that the pathways to learning are varied in both experience and context; they also point to the importance of realms of embodied and situated cognition that are predominantly unconscious, nonverbal, or nonlexical, as well as nonformal or nonpropositional.[24]

Anthropologist, semiotician, and systems thinker Gregory Bateson theorized learning as a general level process, in part because he saw the phenomena entailed within learning to lie at the intersection of many different disciplines (anthropology, biology, psychology, sociology). In his early approach, Bateson distinguished between what he referred to as "proto" and "deutero" learning. By proto learning, Bateson referred to the particulars of "what and how" in learning—the specific content or procedure of something. Through deutero learning, Bateson highlighted the overall broader context of learning. He suggested that while we engage in proto learning, we also learn something about the world in which we are situated more broadly—the overall "attitudes and habits that connect to learning" can become either reinforced or challenged.[25] What Bateson was not evoking here was a linear hierarchy of learning. Rather, he was theorizing that we cannot fully divorce the what of learning from a broader why of learning—for better or worse. In a worst-case scenario, a student who is simply told to memorize facts or to repeat certain movements because they are presented as absolute truths of some kind might simply learn that such facts are rather meaningless and fully set apart from himself. In other words, the student can feel fully divorced from the broader field of learning, that they have nothing to contribute and they cannot be part of the social class of experts—a feeling that many minority students, for example, are left with in paradigmatic learning contexts (natural sciences, honours seminars) that tend to have the highest proportion of white males in esteemed positions.

One of the main points to take from Bateson's theorization is simply the recognition that learning doesn't "come for free," given that each learner is a living being who is bound to engage with broader questions of meaning that cannot be fully predicted—the deutero aspect of learning is particularly emergent in nature and should be respected as such. One distinct way of gaining this recognition would be to lessen the *predetermined* cultural authority of science—in a word, *scientism*—by recognizing that each expert is still figuring things out for themselves. Specifically, if a professor is (or claims to be) part of a community where scholarship is being actively produced, such a professor must on some level be engaged in further learning given that no knowledge community is stable.[26] I suggest that this is indeed what it means to be engaged in "scholarly teaching"; it is to be part of a knowledge community that is actively working on a set of questions and problems, whether they be material (anatomical, cellular, chemical) or more explicitly abstractive (mathematical or philosophical). Again, we can highlight scientific communities as a case example of the fact that such expert communities will keep revisiting, revising, and re-examining both the nature of knowledge and the nature of existence. No scientific, scholarly, or other form of knowledge will ever be completed. As a result, by the very definition of being part of any knowledge community— which is a central way for making a claim for expertise and/or authority—each expert must also remain open to such broader processes of re-evaluation and continued learning.

By more readily recognizing such an open-ended process of knowledge production, we indeed might culturally and socially shift the overall message (the deutero aspect in Bateson's words) of what learning something means. Rather than evoking the all-too-common feeling that learning is a passive process that fully separates the learners and experts, we might cultivate more curiosity (and creativity) if we foreground in our teaching the fact that most questions do remain open for further examination—that the experts do know something but that there is also always room for further engagement. As part of this shift, learning becomes more distinctly co-learning as attention is shifted into both teachers and students to be engaged in further understanding; "We learn nothing from those who say: 'Do as I do.' Our only teachers are those who tell us to 'do with me' and they are able to emit signs to be developed in heterogeneity rather than propose gestures for us to reproduce."[27] To put this differently, the uptakes and applications of teaching cannot and should not be controlled—mimicry does not constitute learning.

One of the ways in which this idea gets articulated in the context of martial arts is that students should (metaphorically, of course) walk a bit behind their teachers but yet never fall into their shadow. I take this expression to mean that as learners we should respect the knowledge of our teachers—in this we recognize they have certain authority—but we also should recognize that we are not our teachers or can become our teachers. As a result, we cannot and should not passively try to copy or imitate from them, because our bodies, our circumstances are not the same. Yet what this does not need to lead into is some utterly solipsistic universe where we all create our own truths, our own facts (the "post-truth" problem). Such solipsism is kept at bay by paying attention to the relationality of our lives—we live in communities of other people and also of other life forms. In other words, if we keep in mind the broader ecology of relations that are part of our learning and teaching, we can better resist the Enlightenment ideals of solipsistic individualism.

Conclusion

This chapter has explored the surprising resonances between martial arts and classroom learning. Just as a martial arts instructor will teach techniques by demonstrating them on every person present in a training session (even on the novice student who is new to the art), an instructor in the classroom might take on the role of student in a much more direct way. We can describe such dynamics in terms of neuronal mirroring: in taijutsu, when an advanced teacher dynamically manipulates a uke's body, practitioners refer to this experience as "getting the feeling" of a technique. This kind of dynamic mirroring is entirely different from the kind of learning that relies upon simply visually observing the movement that another person demonstrates. What this does in the context of martial arts learning is to keep the overall process of cultivating a given somatic tradition an ongoing and dynamic process, one that always involves a broad range of differing body types and one that is open for emergence. Consequently, the learning process is done communally and collectively, while teachers are still recognized as having a certain authority. Importantly, the teachers gain such authority by actively continuing their own study of the art, for example, by travelling to Japan each year in order to enhance their understanding of the art, as well as by actively forming and maintaining the global community of practitioners. On the other hand, if a teacher simply keeps doing the same thing from year to year, they are not regarded with much authority within the overall global community of taijutsu practitioners because when a teacher stops studying and developing, they have set themselves apart from this community.

As a whole, I suggest in this chapter that one of the key aspects that such a dynamic approach to teaching and learning does is help balance two key pedagogical aspects: 1) that there are people who have more expertise and should thereby be granted certain authority; and 2) the expertise of a teacher has no permanence and therefore cannot be absolute—teachers are and should be engaged in further learning. This is in part what defines them as teachers, or, in the context of academia, what "scholarly teaching" in particular can be defined as meaning.

The overall broader key insights that this analysis offers for education in the context of academia, including science, are the following: first, while the authority of experts, particularly as members of a knowledge *community*, needs to be recognized, it is important to resist the draw of foregrounding such authority too much. Naturally, such authority can be very appealing for the experts and the state system at large, yet it can only lead into grand disappointments when no system of knowledge can actually provide certainty. Furthermore, when the expert's authority is foregrounded too much, the deutero learning aspect that Gregory Bateson theorized will easily tilt toward a distinctly disenchanted experience for the students. After all, why would memorization or even understanding matter if someone, somewhere, has it all figured out? On the other hand, and second, if we were to actually teach more in line with the ways in which the originator of taijutsu, Masaaki Hatsumi, approaches movement, highlighting that his art is a living art, one that will keep changing from decade to decade, even on some level year to year, we might be more likely to cultivate a more engaged approach toward knowledge.

NOTES

1. Paolo Freire, *The Pedagogy of the Oppressed* (New York: Continuum, 1970).

2. See Wiebe E. Bijker, "Constructing Worlds: Reflections on Science, Technology and Democracy (and a Plea for Bold Modesty)," *Engaging Science, Technology, and Society* 3 (2017); Jonathan Marks, *Why I Am Not a Scientist: Anthropology and Modern Knowledge* (Berkeley: University of California Press, 2009).

3. Fritjof Crapja and Pier Luigi Luisi, *The Systems View of Life: A Unifying Vision* (Cambridge, MA: Cambridge University Press, 2014).

4. Harry Hubball, Marion L. Pearson, and Anthony Clarke, "SoTL Inquiry in Broader Curricular and Institutional Contexts: Theoretical Underpinnings and Emerging Trends," *Teaching and Learning Inquiry* 1.1 (2013).

5. Priska Schoenborn and Terri Rees, "A Module Designed with Chaos and Complexity in Mind," *Innovations in Teaching & Learning in Information & Computer Sciences* 12.1 (2013).

6. Gary Poole and Nancy Chick, "On the Nature of Expertise in SoTL," *Teaching & Learning Inquiry* 4.2 (2016).

7. Timothy Ingold, "Culture on the Ground: The World Perceived through the Feet," *Journal of Material Culture* 9.3 (2004).

8. Evan Thompson, *Mind in Life: Biology, Phenomenology, and the Science of Mind* (Cambridge, MA: Harvard University Press, 2007).

9. Margaret M. Lock and Nancy Scheper-Hughes, "The Mindful Body: A Prolegomenon to Future Work in Medical Anthropology," *Medical Anthropology Quarterly* 1 (1987); Shigehisa Kuriyama, *The Expressiveness of the Body and the Divergence of Greek and Western Medicine* (New York: Zone, 2002).

10. Drew Leder, *The Absent Body* (Chicago: University of Chicago Press, 1990), 1.

11. Eiko Ikegami, *The Taming of the Samurai: Honorific Individualism and the Making of Modern Japan* (Cambridge, MA: Harvard University Press, 1997).

12. David Abram, *Becoming Animal: An Earthly Cosmology* (New York: Pantheon, 2010), 7.

13. Abram, 8.

14. See Katja Pettinen, "Distributed Addiction: On the Affective Dimensions of Empiricism," in *Semiotics 2012: Semiotics and the New Media*, ed. Leonard G. Brocchi (Ottawa: Legas, 2012).

15. Paul Grobstein, "Revisiting Science in Culture: Science as Story Telling and Story Revising," *Journal of Research Practice* 1.1 (2005).

16. See Lorraine Daston and Peter Galison, *Objectivity* (New York: Zone, 2007).

17. David Hay, Saranne Weller, and Kim Ashton, "Researcher-led Teaching: Embodiment of Academic Practice," *Higher Education Reviews* 48 (2015).

18. Marcelo Gleiser, *The Island of Knowledge: The Limits of Science and the Search for Meaning* (New York: Basic Books, 2014).

19. Timothy Ingold, "Stories against Classification: Transport, Wayfaring and the Integration of Knowledge," in *Kinship and Beyond: The Genealogical Model Reconsidered*, ed. Sandra Bamford and James Leach (Oxford: Berghahn, 2009).

20. Katja Pettinen, "From Habits of Doing to Habits of Feeling: Skill Acquisition in Taijutsu Practice," in *The Encultured Brain: An Introduction to Neuroanthropology*, ed. Daniel Lende and Greg Downey (Cambridge, MA: MIT Press, 2012).

21. Greg Downey, "'Practice without Theory': A Neuroanthropological Perspective on Embodied Learning," *Journal of the Royal Anthropological Institute* 16 (2010); Trevor H.J. Marchand, "Making Knowledge: Explorations of the Indisoluble Relation between Minds, Bodies, and Environment," *Journal of the Royal Anthropological Institute* 16 (2010); Loïc Wacquant, *Body and Soul: Notebooks of an Apprentice Boxer* (New York: Oxford University Press, 2004).

22. Timothy Ingold, *The Perception of the Environment: Essays on Livelihood, Dwelling and Skill* (London: Routledge, 2000); George Lakoff and Mark Johnson, *Philosophy in the Flesh: The Embodied Mind and Its Challenge to Western Thought* (New York: Basic, 1999); Thompson, *Mind in Life*.

23. Mathew Crawford, *The World Beyond Your Head: On Becoming an Individual in an Age of Distraction* (New York: Farrar, Straus and Giroux, 2015); Merlin Donald, *A Mind So Rare: The Evolution of Human Consciousness* (New York: Norton, 2001); Alva Noë, *Out of Our Heads: Why You Are Not Your Brain, and Other Lessons from the Biology of Consciousness* (New York: Hill and Wang, 2009).

24. Greg Downey, "Seeing with a 'Sideways Glance': Visuomotor 'Knowing' and the Plasticity of Perception," in *Ways of Knowing: Anthropological Approaches to Crafting Experience and Knowledge*, ed. Mark Harris (New York: Berghahn, 2007); Kathryn Linn Geurts, *Culture and the Senses: Bodily Ways of Knowing in an African Community* (Berkeley: University of California Press, 2002); Cristina Grasseni, introduction to *Skilled Visions: Between Apprenticeship and Standards*, ed. Cristina Grasseni (New York: Berghahn, 2007); Trevor H.J. Marchand, *The Masons of Djenné* (Bloomington: Indiana University Press, 2009).

25. Peter Felten, "Principles of Good Practice in SoTL," *Teaching and Learning Inquiry* 1.1 (2013): 122.

26. Thomas Kuhn, *The Structure of Scientific Revolutions* (Chicago: University of Chicago Press, 1962).

27. Gilles Deleuze, *Difference and Repetition*, trans. Paul Patton (New York: Columbia University Press, 1994), 22–23.

WORKS CITED

Abram, David. *Becoming Animal: An Earthly Cosmology*. New York: Pantheon, 2010.

Bateson, Gregory. *Steps to an Ecology of Mind*. New York: Ballantine, 1972.

Bijker, Wiebe E. "Constructing Worlds: Reflections on Science, Technology and Democracy (and a Plea for Bold Modesty)." *Engaging Science, Technology, and Society* 3 (2017): 315–31.

Crapja, Fritjof, and Pier Luigi Luisi. *The Systems View of Life: A Unifying Vision*. Cambridge, MA: Cambridge University Press, 2014.

Crawford, Mathew. *The World Beyond Your Head: On Becoming an Individual in an Age of Distraction*. New York: Farrar, Straus and Giroux, 2015.

Daston, Lorraine, and Peter Galison. *Objectivity*. New York: Zone, 2007.

Deleuze, Gilles. *Difference and Repetition*. Translated by Paul Patton. New York: Columbia University Press, 1994.

Donald, Merlin. *A Mind So Rare: The Evolution of Human Consciousness*. New York: Norton, 2001.

Downey, Greg. "'Practice without Theory': A Neuroanthropological Perspective on Embodied Learning." *Journal of the Royal Anthropological Institute* 16 (2010): S22–S40.

——. "Seeing with a 'Sideways Glance': Visuomotor 'Knowing' and the Plasticity of Perception." In *Ways of Knowing: Anthropological Approaches to Crafting Experience and Knowledge*, edited by Mark Harris, 202–24. New York: Berghahn, 2007.

Felten, Peter. "Principles of Good Practice in SoTL." *Teaching and Learning Inquiry* 1.1 (2013): 121–25.

Freire, Paolo. *The Pedagogy of the Oppressed*. New York: Continuum, 1970.

Geurts, Kathryn Linn. *Culture and the Senses: Bodily Ways of Knowing in an African Community*. Berkeley: University of California Press, 2002.

Gleiser, Marcelo. *The Island of Knowledge: The Limits of Science and the Search for Meaning*. New York: Basic Books, 2014.

Grasseni, Cristina. Introduction to *Skilled Visions: Between Apprenticeship and Standards*. Edited by Cristina Grasseni, 1–22. New York: Berghahn, 2007.

Grobstein, Paul. "Revisiting Science in Culture: Science as Story Telling and Story Revising." *Journal of Research Practice* 1.1 (2005): Article M1.

Hay, David, Saranne Weller, and Kim Ashton. "Researcher-led Teaching: Embodiment of Academic Practice." *Higher Education Reviews* 48 (2015): 25–39.

Hubball, Harry, Marion L. Pearson, and Anthony Clarke. "SoTL Inquiry in Broader Curricular and Institutional Contexts: Theoretical Underpinnings and Emerging Trends." *Teaching and Learning Inquiry* 1.1 (2013): 41–57.

Ikegami, Eiko. *The Taming of the Samurai: Honorific Individualism and the Making of Modern Japan*. Cambridge, MA: Harvard University Press, 1997.

Ingold, Timothy. "Culture on the Ground: The World Perceived through the Feet." *Journal of Material Culture* 9.3 (2004): 315–40.

——. *The Perception of the Environment: Essays on Livelihood, Dwelling and Skill*. London: Routledge, 2000.

————. "Stories against Classification: Transport, Wayfaring and the Integration of Knowledge." In *Kinship and Beyond: The Genealogical Model Reconsidered*, edited by Sandra Bamford and James Leach, 193–213. Oxford: Berghahn, 2009.

Kuhn, Thomas. *The Structure of Scientific Revolutions*. Chicago: University of Chicago Press, 1962.

Kuriyama, Shigehisa. *The Expressiveness of the Body and the Divergence of Greek and Western Medicine*. New York: Zone, 2002.

Lakoff, George, and Mark Johnson. *Philosophy in the Flesh: The Embodied Mind and Its Challenge to Western Thought*. New York: Basic, 1999.

Leder, Drew. *The Absent Body*. Chicago: University of Chicago Press, 1990.

Lock, Margaret M., and Nancy Scheper-Hughes. "The Mindful Body: A Prolegomenon to Future Work in Medical Anthropology." *Medical Anthropology Quarterly* 1 (1987): 6–41.

Marchand, Trevor H.J. "Making Knowledge: Explorations of the Indisoluble Relation between Minds, Bodies, and Environment." *Journal of the Royal Anthropological Institute* 16 (2010): S1–S21.

————. *The Masons of Djenné*. Bloomington: Indiana University Press, 2009.

Marks, Jonathan. *Why I Am Not a Scientist: Anthropology and Modern Knowledge*. Berkeley: University of California Press, 2009.

Noë, Alva. *Out of Our Heads: Why You Are Not Your Brain, and Other Lessons from the Biology of Consciousness*. New York: Hill and Wang, 2009.

Pettinen, Katja. "Distributed Addiction: On the Affective Dimensions of Empiricism." In *Semiotics 2012: Semiotics and the New Media*, edited by Leonard G. Brocchi, 97–103. Ottawa: Legas, 2012.

————. "From Habits of Doing to Habits of Feeling: Skill Acquisition in Taijutsu Practice." In *The Encultured Brain: An Introduction to Neuroanthropology*, edited by Daniel Lende and Greg Downey, 195–212. Cambridge, MA: MIT Press, 2012.

Poole, Gary, and Nancy Chick. "On the Nature of Expertise in SoTL." *Teaching & Learning Inquiry* 4.2 (2016): 1–4.

Schoenborn, Priska, and Terri Rees. "A Module Designed with Chaos and Complexity in Mind." *Innovations in Teaching & Learning in Information & Computer Sciences* 12.1 (2013): 14–26.

Thompson, Evan. *Mind in Life: Biology, Phenomenology, and the Science of Mind*. Cambridge, MA: Harvard University Press, 2007.

Wacquant, Loïc. *Body and Soul: Notebooks of an Apprentice Boxer*. New York: Oxford University Press, 2004.

Modes of Hearing
in Music Appreciation

GUY OBRECHT

On Hearing Musical Elements

When we hear something, it is often thought that we are passive receivers of
the information we hear. I'm sitting in a room and I hear a car drive by or an
office chair's creaking and the plastic clacking of my keyboard as I select keys.
But in all of those cases I'm hearing "things," not sounds, and in so far as I know
them as things, then I'm actively hearing them within an ecology of things.[1] That
is, the sounds don't come to us with a label on them, we come to sounds with
an active ear that "finds" elements and deals with them according to a world
of sounds in which they reside. The same is true when we listen to music: we
actively enter into the sound and hear things that the music affords; things like
ideas, feelings, movements, and so on. This chapter is about how I developed a
course that would try to lead students toward developing an ear for hearing the
many ways of understanding music. Through developing these conceptual tools
and trying to get students to apply them to "their own" music, I found the tools
themselves were indicative of a way of hearing that is particular to art-music.
Because of that particularity, I am now better equipped to understand the ideology of popular music consumption and the radical difference that such a mode
of hearing presents to hearing as a critical component of the liberal arts.

Unblocking "Music Appreciation"

Three years ago I started to teach music to undergraduates at Mount Royal University in Calgary, Alberta. I had been teaching music history and music theory to students in the music diploma program for five years prior to this time, but when that department was shuttered I began teaching non-music majors. The change in the student body meant a dramatic change in how I organized and presented the material. When I was in a music department, there was a pretty clear curriculum for both music history and music theory. The former has a series of canonical texts that move through historical periods, presenting an agreed-upon cross-section of representative works and issues in the field, while the latter has basic techniques for the harmonic analysis of music that requires two years of coursework to become fluent in before moving on to more advanced analytical techniques or critical engagement. Both history and theory are considered to be a requirement for the general musical literacy that provides a foundation for the student's growth as a musician and for potential graduate study in musicology. Moving from music students to those from other departments coming to fulfill a general liberal arts requirement meant I could not bring the pedagogical imperatives of musicianship or the assumed understanding of music jargon from the field with me, and as a result I had to rethink both my teaching practice and the course curriculum.

The curriculum I was teaching was developed from scratch. The "shell" course was to be filled with material reflecting the unique research interests of the instructor. This interest was to serve as the course theme, and the content needed to touch on several areas: four historical eras, some non-Western content, and at least one complete text that is considered important to a general understanding of the liberal arts. Since my interest has always been in the phenomenology of music, I chose "music, order, and the ineffable" as my theme, one that would open up ideas for an embodied understanding and pedagogy. My initial version of the course proceeded as a kind of selective history class, starting with medieval era chants and moving through the Renaissance, early modern, and modern eras. The non-Western component was made up of a short detour into the world of Peking Opera, and my text was Nietzsche's early essay, *The Birth of Tragedy*.[2] The class went pretty well, but in terms of the curriculum, I felt it was a little too similar to a light history class. We spent a little too much time in the Renaissance and had to limit our study of contemporary music as a result. The move into Peking Opera felt a little artificial. Lastly, I felt the pre-modern music was a little too inaccessible for a contemporary freshman undergraduate student. So I was left with the challenge of how to incorporate the non–Western, include the contemporary, and have something that was more accessible at the beginning of the class.

The customary approach to teaching music history is to group together examples from a composer: a unit on Romantic era music might begin with Beethoven, looking at his major works, then move on to Schubert, then Brahms, and so on. By presenting material in this way, we are grouping the relevant Romantic composers and their individual works. The argument for this approach is that students will be better able to witness the commonalities that constitute the individual composer's style, as well as those of the era. Yet there is research that suggests we do not learn well from looking at a whole bunch of exemplars of similar phenomena. Kornell and Bjork found that students were better able to recognize an author of a painting if it had been presented not as a block of examples by that author but as one interleaved with others.[3] This logic seems counterintuitive; even the subjects who fared better on the test thought that blocking was the right way to present the information, because we think that the invariant aspect of a style needs to be isolated from other examples in order to pop out and be selectable. But apparently this is not the case, and the result is that many disciplines are thinking about the order and manner in which information is delivered.[4]

The idea of using an element other than chronology to structure a history course is not new. The question is how you organize the material. Reverse chronological organization is possible, ensuring that you get the contemporary music, but the other issues would remain. Grouping by genre is also possible, except that, with the exception of the opera, very few genres in the Western tradition have lasted, and even the opera only goes back to the beginning of modernity. Themes are another possibility, but getting a theme that is not too broad or too temporally fixed proves to be challenging. My solution was to use "musical elements" as the structural backdrop of the class, a reasoning that assumed the elements of music are really tools that let us talk about any kind of music. Normally, these elements are considered background knowledge or are given as a prelude to the less informed reader in a listening course.[5] This approach solved the three concerns I had with the first course: it allowed me to bring up contemporary music as much as ancient; it allowed me to include non–Western examples alongside Western ones; and it allowed me to include accessible and less accessible music in the same day.

The "interleaved" version of the course took seven elements (timbre, texture, harmony, rhythm, metre, melody, and form) and used each one as a "way in" to talking about musical examples from the ages. For example, with timbre (the unique sound of an instrument, including levels of amplitude, types of attack, and pitch), we considered how timbres could inform the consecration of the Florentine Cathedral, how they represent narrative space in early opera of the seventeenth century, how voice types represent power in *opera seria* of the eighteenth century, how the orchestra presents one or several soloists, and how the scientific understanding of timbre gets poetized in the twentieth century in experimental compositions. Timbre can even be taken into the significance of the animal hide from which the drum and mallet are made in different Indigenous nations and the sound of the voice in Peking Opera. Thus, the students were introduced to the ways in which different composers and cultures used timbre to make meaningful compositions that spoke to the technological developments and philosophical understandings of their time.

I arranged the elements in the order of what I considered to be our most immediate engagement with music: starting with timbre, then rhythm and metre, then melody and harmony, and finishing with form. I removed texture after the first run-through because it is such a particularly Western-centric way of looking at music and it can be covered in a discussion of melody. By starting with the most phenomenally present aspect of music, the sound, and moving toward higher orderings, harmony and form, I felt the course would be well positioned to engage even the most musically illiterate students and invite them to witness how music can define an age and provide insight into how a historically situated understanding of humanity is refracted and articulated through cultural products.

Embodied Pedagogy: How We Hear with Our Bodies

Having developed a curriculum suited to the general liberal arts student, I now had to adjust the way I actually delivered or taught the elements. Most of the students had little or no musical background, so I needed to explain things like "pitch," "scale," "beat," "consonance," and "functional harmony" before using them to talk about the larger elements and particular compositions. Of course, there are mathematical definitions of most musical things, perfect ratios for consonance, pitch as a frequency, the chromatic pitch set as a frequency set defined by the twelfth root of two, beat as a BPM ratio, and so on. While I am comfortable introducing students to this kind of a definition, it is meaningless without knowing the experience. When dealing with a music student, they already "know" what a pitch is because they have tuned their instruments and played melodies (even most percussionists have some experience working with pitches if not pitch sets), so explaining a mathematical or physical definition is another way of understanding that experience.[6] When trying to explain these concepts to non-music students in an effort to direct their listening, explaining it via physics and math seems a little bit like the famous thought experiment that highlights the difference between experiencing and knowing a colour.[7] In order to explain these concepts, I use a "triangulated" approach: know it in the abstract, know it in the body, know it in the literature (via musical examples).

The most obviously embodied musical element is rhythm/metre. Dividing a beat into two or three parts is conceptually a basic fraction, but when we hear rhythm, we do not "hear" fractions, we hear motion that is understood with the body. When a toddler bounces to music, she is "sketching" the beat with her body; when we dance, we are illustrating our understanding of the metric motion of the music with our bodies and thus showing "how we hear" with our bodies. In terms of "hearing as," or Wittgenstein's notion of aspect-perception, our hearing is usually based in an understanding of the moving body: *now* it sounds like a dance, *now* it sounds like a march.[8] For example, when we understand the tempo of a beat, we understand it as a motion of the body, which is why musical tempos fall within the range of the body's speeds; a "fast" tempo corresponds to the speed of running, a slow tempo to that of a leisurely stroll. The metre, or grouping of beats, is accomplished through distinguishing a particular beat, aligning one's breath with a group of two beats, skipping a beat, and so on.

For the triangulated approach, I first illustrate the creation of a beat as a schematic of points, talk about the relation to dance forms and modern day BPMs. I use a computer to show different paces and groupings in the abstract (a simple beat box patch written with the graphic programming interface PureData[9]). In order to teach the element of rhythm in the body, students are given exercises in the class of clapping or tapping a beat and creating different beat groups via a variety of techniques like emphasizing a beat, alternating the method of producing it (snaps, taps, thumps, and so on), or moving in tandem to a larger beat grouping. Finally, we start to associate the beat with particular pieces of music. Classical ballet is perfect for this exercise because it "wears its metre on its sleeve" in order that various dance exercises and types can be choreographed. Students are asked to clap the beat and the metre of various examples.

With this understanding of rhythm and metre, we are able to look at examples of art music that obscure the beat (the polyphonic fifteenth-century mass, the madrigal, monody, the eighteenth-century dance suites made for listening, and modern experimental music). In all of these cases, the lack of clarity in the metre is an aspect of the piece that tells us about the meaning of the piece in relation to its day. For example, perhaps a clear metre would not be appropriate for worship because God is not to be addressed in human terms, or worship is done from a point of stillness. The madrigal uses a fluctuating metre to represent elements of the text that it is setting, slowing down when talking about sadness or a long sigh, or becoming regular to represent a body pacing back and forth (as is the case with Monteverdi's madrigal, "The Nymph's Lament"[10]). For monody, the student can think about how the lack of danceable or regular rhythm corresponds to the natural rhythm of speech delivered in a heightened dramatic mode that is representative of particular affective states. For the eighteenth-century dance suites, the student can now see how something that was meant for dancing has become something that is *about* dancing, that is, something that rehearses a kind of historical knowledge or a musical historical discourse. In the modern era, the student can appreciate how minimalist experiments with metric ratios and the quest for transcendent music embodies a modernist ethos. In the end, with a little bit of understanding of the metrical aspect of music, the student can enter into a sophisticated understanding of the manifold ways that music has been used in the past six centuries.

That metre is based in the body is easy enough to understand: consider the original Latin term for tempo, *tactus*; that is, touch. But the other elements? Timbre? Melody? Harmony? Form? When I talk about timbre, I consider the term broadly to include pitch, attack, and dynamics, along with a discussion of the harmonic series and resonant frequencies. Normally, pitch and dynamics are considered part of something a little more proper to music theory, but I use it as "sound" because the students do not need or necessarily have any musical theory knowledge; I include it in this element as a "musical sound." But even the most scientific understanding of sound comes back to the body. I begin by introducing students to the idea that they are already experts at identifying timbres—a point noted by Daniel Levitin, that, within milliseconds of hearing the opening guitar tones from the Eagles' song "Hotel California," they can identify it.[11] This ability to identify a song is not because the song is particularly original in its first few hundred milliseconds; it is perhaps a couple of tones from a B-minor chord. The identity is from the timbre of the chord played on that guitar in that recording context, and it is that rich array of information that we are already experts at identifying. This is a skill that is deeply ingrained in us as mammals who are in tune with our environment, knowing what is around us by associating the unique timbral signatures of its presence, and as social animals, we need to know who is who. Of course, our unique identity, our voice, comes from the physiological properties of the body, the size and shape of bodily cavities, and the way in which we navigate those cavities. From low notes that use our chest to high notes that use our head, our voice "sits" in our body, and how we attack the vocal chords with our breath controls what we sound like, and, of course, it has an effect on how we try to say what we want to say—"I didn't mean to say *THAT*; I meant *this*!" From here we can begin to look at how instruments become extensions of this same voice, utilizing different tools and techniques to exploit an understanding of the sonorous possibilities of the instrument, be they in columns of air or strings on a sound board. We can note further that, in fact, instrumental families are defined less by their sound than by the way our bodies interact with them—the fingering of woodwind instruments, keyboards, and strings is such that if you know how to play one you can usually make sounds on the others in the family.

This embodied understanding is supported by an abstract tone generator that illustrates what oscillator waves "look like" and how manipulating the amplitudes of particular elements of groups of oscillators produces different timbres. This "scientific" understanding of timbre is used as the foundation for exploratory pieces of twentieth-century music like Alvin Lucier's *Vespers* and *I Am Sitting in a Room*.[12] *Vespers* introduces students to the problem or idea of animal awareness by challenging performers to use echolocation to define their environments, but also allows reflection on the nature of timbre as something functional to human consciousness. As an added bonus, students can actually perform *Vespers* with a follow-up discussion of the experience of timbre and place. With *I Am Sitting in a Room*, students are introduced to the idea of resonant frequencies in rooms. The recursive recording and rerecording can be accomplished quite easily with a computer, so the students can replicate the piece in their particular classrooms. Timbre can also function at the symbolic level, revealing a recurrent theme or object in an opera (like the magic flute and bells in Mozart's *Magic Flute*). Even further back in history, timbre functions at the rhetorical level, for example in Monteverdi's *Orfeo* when Orfeus tries to manipulate the underworld with his musical powers: we understand that he is convincing the various gods and demons through the fact that more instruments begin to join him.[13] That is, timbre supports the rhetorical process of the argument. Lastly, we look at examples of timbre in madrigals and motets of the Renaissance that illustrate the nature of the text—for example, madrigals that use high pitches to illustrate stars and low pitches to illustrate the earth, as in Monteverdi's "Sfogava con le stelle."[14] Students are thus brought to understand how timbre can be used in ways that are unique to, and reflect the values of, their time, from a pre-Enlightenment "similitude" of sound representations to a modern scientific perspective of sound waves in space.

Because the understanding of timbre is sufficiently broad-based to include pitch frequency and amplitude, the move to melody does not require much more than the presentation of pitch sets and the application of rhythm. In terms of understanding melodic motion, students are presented with the idea of "leaping" or "stepwise" motion that is either ascending or descending; our melodic understanding is still based in a body that moves in the world. Of particular interest to the understanding of melody, so central to our recollections of music and musical identity, is the idea that a melody can, in itself, somehow have meaning. The idea of melody having a fixed meaning is central to the notion of chant, whereby the presentation of the chant melody is supposed to carry the sacred meaning into whatever context it is put—the musical concept known as the "paraphrase." The paraphrase technique is contrasted to melodic "pictures" that are created in madrigals, where melodic meaning is created through move-ment in relation to the text. Melody in the context of early monody is similarly connected to the text, but the monodist is interested in how it is delivered, thus representing how the elocution of the text is central to its meaning—the paralinguistic elements or the *way* that something is said determines its expres-sive content. In the eighteenth century, melodies begin to represent "character types" by using styles that have different historical and contextual connections, from simple and short for "simpletons," to long and enlightened for thoughtful and logical heroines, to pompous and ridiculous or illogical and outrageous.[15] Melodies become the vehicle for a particular understanding of character. In the nineteenth century, melodies begin to tell stories, culminating in the music dramas of Wagner that use leitmotifs to develop a narrative. And, finally, in the twentieth century, the melodic underpinning gets pulled and, once again, a scientific or "set theoretic" approach to melody becomes the norm. Once again, students are given a tour of how a musical element, melody, has been used in many different ways to meaningfully speak of and to the underlying philosophy of their age.

For harmony, I begin with Tinctoris's sixteenth-century counterpoint treatise,[16] wherein he places the qualities of consonance and dissonance in our understanding of relations with people—that is, consonant intervals characterize a good relationship, and dissonant intervals speak to some kind of disagreement or friction. Thus, harmony begins in social relations and bodily feeling, and once students understand the rudimentary mathematics of intervals, I present them with harmonic intervals of varying qualities. For music, they are now primed to understand the dominance of consonance in the contrapuntal textures of the Renaissance mass, where the consonance forms the pillars that maintain careful control of dissonance. Then we look at madrigals where dissonance is treated freely in the context of representing some painful element of the text (loss, sadness, pain, tears, and so on). Similarly, we can talk to the expressive use of dissonance in early seventeenth-century monody by returning to Monteverdi's *Orfeo* and examining the reaction of Orfeus to the news of his wife's death. For understanding how functional harmony (the syntactical use of consonance and dissonance to establish and prolong the sense of resolution or return), I turn again to Vivaldi and then Mozart, the masters of harmonic progression and the frustration of return. Functional harmony can be taught by having students stand until the music resolves or through a game of musical chairs where instead of waiting for the music to turn off they wait until the cadence changes. For the extended harmony of the nineteenth century, I return to Wagner, this time playing the Tristan chord. With a little understanding of harmony under their belts, they are easily able to point to the fact that it is a highly dissonant chord and the various resolutions of it are good but lacking in a sense of real resolve. This understanding can then complement the idea of the leitmotif telling a story of unrequited love out of a harmony that "sounds" as if it is impossible from the outset. This situation sets the stage for the discussion of the twentieth century, where dissonance is "emancipated" in the new compositions of the second Viennese school, and resolution is removed as a requisite feature of a composition in modern experimental music.

Putting It All Together

With the unblocked approach to music listening, I hope to show students how the elements of music have been put to remarkably different uses in ways that reflect philosophical understandings of the nature of being and expression, theories of social order, and the natural physical world. Students experience the works·in an active way, thinking about what the work has to say from multiple perceptual frames, but they also experience them as musical phenomena. Part of my pedagogical plan in returning to the same work over the course of the semester is to eventually "put it back together" as a work that is experienced in a way that is at once holistic and also indeterminate. That is, students should come to see that there are many ways that a work can address them, and many ways that they can address it. Ultimately, it was my hope that, given these listening tools, students could begin to use them to consider the kinds of things that are happening in the music with which they are familiar. For their end of term assignment, I asked them to choose a piece of music from their contemporary experience and explain their understanding of it through a consideration of the materials that it uses (timbres, harmony, metre, and melody). Theoretically, this assignment seems consistent: learn how conceptual listening tools work in different musical compositions, realize that musical experience can be multifaceted, and then apply this realization to new experiences of music that are not part of the course content. This idea of theoretical consistency, however, neglected to consider that the analytical "tools" have a particular application that is geared toward a particular outcome.

Initially, it was my thinking that "music is music" and that "melodic motion and harmony are recurring elements in music." Therefore, I thought, it follows that one can consider the musical elements to think about any particular piece of music—the elements will not tell you everything about it, but they will tell you something. The error in this reasoning is that it assumes that musical elements, being universal to music (a slightly questionable claim in itself), are somehow going to support one's understanding. The papers I received over the two semesters that I used this assignment challenged this assumption. The papers usually pointed out how the artist under discussion was important to students for some reason. For example, the artist may have showed them how to overcome some difficulty in their life, like parents getting a divorce, a family member getting in an accident, a time when they were bullied, a relationship that ended, or some similarly traumatic experience. In other cases, the artists were sources of pure inspiration, true kinds of muses, because they did everything with such perfection and overcame the odds, or hung onto their particular visions. Other papers, in a slightly similar vein, described how the music was being used to "get pumped up" before a game or a workout or to frame some kind of recreational activity. The "uses" of music seemed to confirm ideas about music as a tool for establishing identity and modulating one's environment that are put forward by scholars like Tia DeNora.[17] Where the papers faltered was in using the musical elements that had been studied in class as tools to unpack and reflect in a critical way upon their use. I hoped that they would be able to support their position with direct reference to the music through the application of the conceptual tools of musical elements. My hopes were dashed.

Initially, I thought the problem was that they were not comfortable talking about the elements they had learned. Even though they had learned that they feel things like rhythm, timbre, and harmony, perhaps they were not well versed enough in the application to be able to take their learning to that level (though it is an early point in Bloom's taxonomy). The papers were often more generally about an artist or genre, and they unfolded in such a way that no evidence was offered for their understanding. My second idea was that, perhaps, because they were not really used to making arguments, period, employing an analysis of musical elements to support one was difficult. In my comments on these papers, I encouraged students to try and unpack their understand-ing of the artist as a hero/mentor, or the genre as inspiration, with particular examples. That is, I asked them to take a particular work and try and think about how its musical elements supported their positions. In my comments, I often pointed to elements of form and harmony and asked them to think about the nature of the expectations that are set up, thwarted, and then delivered, or not, as the case may be: What does it mean that a song has no harmonic motion or narrative trajectory? How does this hyperfast tempo relate to your activities? And so on. In many cases, where students had pointed to songs without doing any analysis, I would listen to those songs and think about how they could have used timbral elements at the very least, thinking about how the "tone of voice" supports their understanding of the artist's story. In some cases, the songs seemed to be referencing pop genres of the past, like '60s rock and roll, or folk rock, or disco, or '80s synth rock. How could this kind of reference support their understanding? Is it ironic or is it authentic and reverent? Surely, I thought, these musical elements could be incorporated into an argument of some form! Surely, I think, I was wrong.

It was while reading Alva Noë's book, *Strange Tools*,[18] that I began to see the error in my assumption that students could take conceptual tools that they learn for addressing and thinking about art music and apply them to pop music. The two music types are actually fundamentally different on an experiential level. That is, we address the experience in different ways. We do not need any abstract musical tools to "get" what is going on in popular music. If you do not immediately "get it," you will not get it later by thinking about its form or place in the history of pop music. Pop music is a completely different mode of address than art music. When we hear popular music, it becomes a direct presentation of a particular artist's style. The music is conceptually transparent to that artist's style; we understand immediately what it is and whether we relate to it without hearing musical elements. For Noë, this is why we often express our understanding through playing air guitar—or some other way of mimicking the action of the performer.[19] It is the subjectivity of the performer that is understood through the music. To try and focus on the musical elements is to move *away* from that understanding and to somehow make something that was transparent become opaque. It is like presenting people with a picture and then asking them to talk about the photographic paper that it is printed on: it is not necessarily unrelated to the picture, and it might even be quite interesting if you are a photographer or a printer, but by and large its nonpresence is what allows us to look at the subject or content of the picture. In pop music we hear "through" the music to the subjectivity and style of the artist in a way that makes the musical elements similarly nonpresent.

Hearing art music does not lead to the immediate understanding of popular music. We may immediately understand that there is something happening, some ordering of the sonic world, but it is not a kind of channel to the subjectivity of the artist in the same way. An initial hearing of a madrigal, for example, will seem to be standing in the way of hearing a particular subjectivity. We hear a colossal group of voices traversing an endless and extreme melody with sudden movement from high to low pitches. We hear different lengths of phrase and rhythmic irregularities. We hear formlessness. Nothing about hearing a madrigal sweeps the listener into the psyche and style of the artist. It stands on its own, in front of us, looking at us for a response, whereas popular music pulls us into its vortex whether or not we want to go there. Art music requires the listener to "assent" before it reveals its content, and that revelation is always an opening to rethink. When we assent to it, we can begin to hear that the madrigal's harmony is connected to the text: dissonance is associated with pain, and phrase endings correspond with line punctuation; its rhythm moves fast when talking about fast things; it breaks into fast imitation when there is a chase; the melody is high when talking about high things; and so on. These are all ways of understanding the text and also the nature of music. It is, in the case of the madrigal, music about music, and with the many genres that followed this kind of self-generating "autopoiesis" quality remains.

In the cases where there is the presentation of music about music, it is possible to utilize an understanding of the musical elements in order to understand what the music is doing. We, in fact, need the tools in order to unpack the content. This circumstance does not mean there is not any kind of visceral engagement with the sound in art music but that the sound itself is the content, and to address that content, we need the tools. Do we have an idea of what Beethoven is doing in the Ninth Symphony if we do not know the history of the genre or the other genres that it uses, like opera? No. That does not mean that knowing the form of a symphony and the flexible rhythm of monody or recitative from the operatic tradition will explain it all; on the contrary, it is in hearing these things that the oddness and the inexplicable come to the foreground of experience. It is precisely at the juncture where art music leaves our understanding of music that it becomes strange and inherently valuable. The conceptual tools allow us to consider ways that art music throws our contemporary perspective into question.

Noë's argument, supported by my music appreciation class, may sound elitist. Surely, there is a genre of pop music out there that has similar elements to art music. Isn't listening a singular activity? And, to a degree, this assertion is true. That is, in the first place, there is popular music that uses art music–like techniques. For example, lots of rap music "samples" sounds from different eras and puts them in a new context. Isn't this the same as hearing how Mozart uses antiquated styles of music to characterize feudalistic characters, or simple melodies to underscore a pretentious buffoon?[20] That is, does the practice of recontextualizing a style make it arty? And I think it is safe to say that, yes, there is an arty element here, but you do not actually need to know the stylistic reference in rap to still get *exactly* what it is about: the rapper's style. Similarly, we could talk about art–pop groups like Pink Floyd or Yes, groups that wrote "concept albums" that used musical elements to tell a story or carry some kind of a narrative. In these cases, there are melodic and thematic returns and developments across larger spans that one could argue are arty in that they are developing meaning through a kind of discourse of musical elements. But here, again, the art element is really acting as a secondary experience to the way we understand the musician—that is, the focus comes back to the style of the artist. Even while there are art music elements in these cases, those elements are not essential to the mode of addressing the music.

I said this might sound elitist, and I think this is how my students normally interpret the conversation: "There goes Obrecht justifying his elite musical tastes again." But "elite" is a problematic term because it implies a kind of pre-enlightened mode of thinking; namely, that there is an arbitrary rule that separates camps and enables a particular faction of society to rise above the rest. Elitism has become a rallying cry of right–wing political campaigns to claim that anything that challenges us to think is a conspiracy of the liberal-minded. This understanding of art music is not elitist in any pre–enlightened, arbitrary rule sense; on the contrary, it is asking that the student resist claims to normative thinking. The new "arbitrary rule" is that everything should be easy to understand, and, if it is not, it is because someone is oppressing you. The ideological position is that art should be confirming who you are without you having to actually do anything. But the act is important: it tells us who we are, it comes up against structural orderings and wrestles with them. It encounters, it has agency, and it discovers who the agent is alongside the incredible masters of the past.[21] There are different ways of hearing, and we should be extremely suspicious of anything that tells us otherwise.

NOTES

1. This "ecological" approach to perception has its roots in James Gibson's theories of visual perception (see *The Ecological Approach to Visual Perception* [Boston: Houghton Mifflin, 1979]) and has been further developed in regards to music by Eric Clarke in *Ways of Listening: An Ecological Approach to the Perception of Musical Meaning* (Oxford: Oxford University Press, 2005).

2. The particularly accessible translation by Walter Kaufman, Friedrich Nietzsche, *The Birth of Tragedy, and the Case of Wagner* (New York: Vintage Books, 1967).

3. Nate Kornell and Robert A. Bjork, "Learning Concepts and Categories: Is Spacing the 'Enemy of Induction'?" *Psychological Science* 19.6 (June 2008).

4. See, for example, Doug Rohrer, "Interleaving Helps Students Distinguish among Similar Concepts," *Educational Psychology Review* 24.3 (September 2012).

5. See, for example, Mark Evan Bonds et al., *Listen to This* (Upper Saddle River, NJ: Prentice Hall, 2011).

6. Not that these kinds of definitions are really all that important for music students learning how to use pitches in practice; more important is learning the relationships that pitches and pitch sets have.

7. Frank Jackson, "Epiphenomenal Qualia," *Philosophical Quarterly* 32.127 (1982).

8. Ludwig Wittgenstein, *Philosophical Investigations*, ed. and trans. G.E.M. Anscombe, P.M.S. Hacker, and Joachim Schulte, rev. 4th ed. (London: Wiley Blackwell, 2009), 217e.

9. PureData is an open source program developed by Miller Puckette.

10. Claudio Monteverdi, "Lamento della Ninfa," *Madrigali dei guerrieri et amorosi* (Venice, Italy: Alessandro Vincenti, 1638).

11. Daniel Levitin, *This Is Your Brain on Music: The Science of a Human Obsession* (New York: Dutton, 2006).

12. Alvin Lucier, *Reflections: Interviews, Scores, Writings* (Germany: MusikTexte, 1995).

13. Claudio Monteverdi, *L'Orfeo: favola in musica for soloists, chorus, and orchestra*, ed. Denis Stevens (Borough Green, UK: Novello, 1968 [1609]).

14. Claudio Monteverdi, "Sfogava con le stelle," *Il Quarto Libro de Madrigali a Cinque Voci* (Venice, Italy: Ricciardo Amadino, 1603).

15. Mozart was a master at using various styles to illustrate characters, from his opera, *The Marriage of Figaro*, to his final dramatic work, *The Magic Flute*. See *Le nozze di Figaro/The Marriage of Figaro: An Opera in Four Acts*, ed. Ruth Martin and Thomas Martin (New York: G. Schirmer, 1951 [1786]); *The Magic Flute: Opera in Two Acts, KV 620*, ed. Gernot Gruber et al. (London: Faber Music, 1984 [1791]). A detailed study

of these kinds of musical characterizations and their use can be found in Bruce Alan Brown, *W.A. Mozart: Cosi fan Tutte* (New York: Cambridge University Press, 1995).

16. Johannes Tinctoris, *The Art of Counterpoint/Liber de arte contrapuncti*, ed. and trans. Albert Seay (New York: American Institute of Musicology, 1961 [1477]).

17. Tia DeNora, *Music in Everyday Life* (New York: Cambridge University Press, 2000).

18. Alva Noë, *Strange Tools: Art and Human Nature* (New York: Hill and Wang, 2015).

19. See Noë's chapter 15, "Air Guitar Styles," in *Strange Tools*.

20. Contrast the Queen of the Night's use of recitative, aria, arioso, in her first act aria, "O zitt're nicht, mein lieber Sohn!"/"Zum Leiden bin ich auserkoren"/"Du wirst sie zu" ("Oh don't tremble, my dear son"/"I am meant for suffering"/"You will go with her"), with Papageno's short, simple, and ridiculous, "Der Vogelfanger bin ich ja" ("A bird catcher that's me") in Mozart's *The Magic Flute*.

21. Matthew B. Crawford, *The World Beyond Your Head: On Becoming an Individual in an Age of Distraction* (New York: Farrar, Straus and Giroux, 2015).

WORKS CITED

Bonds, Mark Evan, Jocelyn R. Neal, Joseph S. Kaminski, and N. Scott Robinson. *Listen to This*. Upper Saddle River, NJ: Prentice Hall, 2011.

Brown, Bruce Alan. *W.A. Mozart: Così fan tutte*. New York: Cambridge University Press, 1995.

Clarke, Eric. *Ways of Listening: An Ecological Approach to the Perception of Musical Meaning*. Oxford: Oxford University Press, 2005.

Crawford, Matthew B. *The World Beyond Your Head: On Becoming an Individual in an Age of Distraction*. New York: Farrar, Straus and Giroux, 2015.

DeNora, Tia. *Music in Everyday Life*. New York: Cambridge University Press, 2000.

Gibson, James J. *The Ecological Approach to Visual Perception*. Boston: Houghton Mifflin, 1979.

Jackson, Frank. "Epiphenomenal Qualia." *Philosophical Quarterly* 32.127 (1982): 127–36.

Kornell, Nate, and Robert A. Bjork. "Learning Concepts and Categories: Is Spacing the 'Enemy of Induction'?" *Psychological Science* 19.6 (June 2008): 585–92.

Levitin, Daniel. *This Is Your Brain on Music: The Science of a Human Obsession*. New York: Dutton, 2006.

Lucier, Alvin. *Reflections: Interviews, Scores, Writings*. Germany: MusikTexte, 1995.

Monteverdi, Claudio. "Lamento della Ninfa." *Madrigali dei guerrieri et amorosi*. Venice, Italy: Alessandro Vincenti, 1638.

———. *L'Orfeo: favola in musica for soloists, chorus, and orchestra*. Edited by Denis Stevens. Borough Green, UK: Novello, 1968 [1609].

———. "Sfogava con le stelle." *Il Quarto Libro de Madrigali a Cinque Voci*. Venice, Italy: Ricciardo Amadino, 1603.

Mozart, Wolfgang A. *Le nozze di Figaro/The Marriage of Figaro: An Opera in Four Acts*. Edited by Ruth Martin and Thomas Martin. New York: G. Schirmer, 1951 [1786].

———. *The Magic Flute: Opera in Two Acts, KV 620*. Edited by Gernot Gruber, Alfred Orel, Heinz Moehn, and Andrew Porter. London: Faber Music, 1984 [1791].

Nietzsche, Friedrich W. *The Birth of Tragedy, and the Case of Wagner*. Translated by Walter Kaufman. New York: Vintage Books, 1967.

Noë, Alva. *Strange Tools: Art and Human Nature*. New York: Hill and Wang, 2015.

Rohrer, Doug. "Interleaving Helps Students Distinguish among Similar Concepts." *Educational Psychology Review* 24.3 (September 2012): 355–67.

Tinctoris, Johannes. *The Art of Counterpoint/Liber de arte contrapuncti*. Edited and translated by Albert Seay. New York: American Institute of Musicology, 1961 [1477].

Wittgenstein, Ludwig. *Philosophical Investigations*. Edited and translated by G.E.M. Anscombe, P.M.S. Hacker, and Joachim Schulte. Revised 4th ed. London: Wiley Blackwell, 2009.

Bruised Tomatoes

KAITLIN ROTHBERGER

> I have come to believe over and over again that what is most
> important to me must be spoken, made verbal and shared,
> even at the risk of having it bruised and misunderstood.
>
> —Audre Lorde, *Sister Outsider*

THIS CHAPTER BEGINS IN A PLACE MANY WOULD LIKE TO AVOID: the contested and open-ended dynamic between students and teachers in undergraduate classrooms. I write this chapter from the perspective of an undergraduate student, seeking to make sense of the dissonant methods at play within classroom spaces. In particular, I am interested in foregrounding the dissonance between two kinds of classrooms: an exhausting classroom and an uplifting classroom. I take cues, in this reflection, from bell hooks's descrip- tion of teaching as a caring profession within a society that devalues all caring professions—"no wonder then that professors, especially those at elite institu- tions, eschew the notion of service as a vital dimension of their work with stu- dents in and out of the classroom."[1] I wonder, could one open up the spaces of learning in ways that disrupt prevailing conventions of what it means to teach and be taught? This question draws attention to the neoliberal "story" and the importance of questioning its presumptions about why and how the classroom experience matters. As Maggie Berg and Barbara K. Seeber write, "We academ- ics should, collectively, talk to each other more about how we actually spend our time, with all the anxieties, displacements, and failures that involves."[2] Caring, I know, is at odds with normalizing, and there are myriad normalizing pressures at work within academia that afflict students and teachers alike, but personal narratives can push our thinking forward, and communal support can disrupt the symptoms of a deeply indoctrinated system.

My own contributions to this conversation are twofold. First, I turn to the metaphor of "tomatoes" that other participants in this collection deploy as a way to describe the design choices and styles that characterize particular teaching practices, and I emphasize an "ingredient" of tomatoes that tends to be overlooked in critical scholarship about undergraduate education, namely the co-constitution of pedagogy between teachers and their students. After all, "tomatoes" only enact their design-conceits because of their interplay with students. The ingredient I explore in this piece concerns this dynamic between teachers and students: I call it "bruised tomatoes." Second, I pay attention to the culinary or vegetative connotations of the metaphor "tomato," opening up the possibility that there are pressing dynamics involving appetite and hunger, taste and conformity in classrooms that deserve sustained attention. My metaphor, "bruised tomatoes," refers to the potential for harm that under-graduate students face in classrooms that are organized around the normalizing dictates of neoliberal universities. It also refers to the significance of claiming one's appetite as a student, embracing the edifying work of bruised tomatoes. The stakes of this discussion are high: Jess Zimmerman names the radical potential that opens up when women claim their appetites, and the isolating shame that comes with wanting to be noticed—"A man's appetite can be hearty, but a woman with an appetite...is always voracious: she always overreaches, because it is not supposed to exist."[3]

Through linking these seemingly divergent areas of thought, I rearticulate the nascent links between pedagogy and mental illness to reimagine woman's role in the undergraduate classroom. What might happen, I ask, if we confronted the rituals of the neoliberal classroom and began to imagine the possibilities of love and care labour in pedagogical scenarios? If we began to speak and to eat where both silence and starvation have been advised and mused, all the while, about the necessary danger of a *bruised* tomato?

Classrooms are never neutral spaces. Indeed, each classroom exerts its own particular structure around how we "see" teaching and learning. It is therefore a critical act to ask: "Whose voices do you see? Whose bodies do you hear?"[4] These questions compel us to recognize that space and action are entangled within classrooms: it is not simply that one acts in particular ways in certain spaces but that one's actions are restricted or compelled by these spaces; classrooms decide, in crucial ways, what may occur or recur within their walls. These two points get at the heart of the "tomato"—of what it means to participate in the design of the classroom.

As Namrata Mitra articulates in her chapter, the tomato of one pedagogical space is very likely in tension with the tomato down the hall. There are shared commonalities, however, across many classrooms. The undergraduate philosophy classroom as I have come to know it, for example, is so often not a cozy space, and its qualities can feel overwhelming because there is nowhere you can escape being implicated in it, by it, and through it. I come to the classroom and to this chapter as a woman with mental illness, and the material effects of this inform my relationship to pedagogy more generally and to the philosophy classroom more specifically. I find myself insisting: yes, I am crazy, but I am smart too, and sometimes it is hard to be both. The tomatoes cultivated in the classroom, both within neoliberal institutions and more contemporary radical teaching practices, so often presuppose a student who is white, neurotypical, and male, and in classrooms such as these I have very calmly gone mad. And so, in keeping with Berg and Seeber's slow professor movement, I am beginning the work of shifting the question from "what is wrong with me" to "what is wrong with the institution of academia"—"What is it about the university system," they wonder, "that makes people feel unable to cope."[5]

We all—students and teachers alike—come to the classroom differently, even when we arrive at the space concurrently. Even those who are *in place* must also arrive *here*, but these arrivals are all too often unnoticed, and it is the out-of-place bodies that are perceived to be disruptive. Phenomenology teaches us that spaces are not wholly exterior to bodies; rather, they are like a "second skin that unfolds in the folds of the body."[6] In her critique of Quineans, those who follow and work on Quine, Lorraine Code writes, "[They] do not engage in analyses of *institutions* of knowledge production. They neither take account of the unequal contributions of different social groups...nor do they consider how allegedly objective value systems can themselves be ideological in character."[7] What needs to be explored is precisely this inability to register difference as it has been inscribed on the flesh, on the mind, and to make room for the sexually specific bodies and the mentally ill bodies and the disabled bodies and the racialized bodies as they come into the classroom space.

In a word, there is a failing of the undergraduate philosophy classroom's vernacular to register another "we." But it is possible to cultivate other ways of relating to and recognizing each other. The tomato I want to endorse is what we could describe as a bruised tomato. As Berg and Seeber point out, "To talk about the body and emotion goes against the grain of an institution that privileges the mind and reason,"[8] and the bruised tomato does precisely this. When the tomato is passed around in ways unimagined—when it is handled by the wrong hands, in the wrong spaces, dropped—we encounter, perhaps for the first time, a certain wild justice to pedagogy. We break harmony with the isolating sorrow of neoliberalism. To be a woman in the classroom is to be reminded, at every turn, of your body, and to experience mental illness is to be submerged in the precarity of performing mental health. In the undergraduate philosophy classroom I have spent the bulk of my time reading texts I was never meant to read, that were never written with me in mind, that do not take my body into account, and this has cultivated within me a certain kind of madness. I am *mad* at school, and I have gone mad *at* school. But the ways the classroom has handled me—has held me and continues to shape me—offer a kind of feedback loop for thinking through the ways *I* can handle, can cope, and embrace: the bruising of a tomato never quite offered me but taken anyway.

The bruised tomato calls forth a raging against "learnification," against the *ad feminam* of philosophy, and against the tacit objectivity of knowledge *proper*. By "learnification," I refer to Gert Biesta's incisive critique of the purportedly student-focused approaches within neoliberal universities. Biesta is dismissive of this kind of student focus because it erases the very play of pedagogical design work and replaces it with standardized, consumerist pre-occupations. "To see learning as something constructed and artificial," writes Biesta, "makes it impossible to expose the political 'work' done through the idea of 'learning.'"[9]

I am sympathetic to the romantic rhetoric of neoliberal individualism, the pull of the disembodied "I," but what we lose in these moments is the opportunity to see the body as a pedagogical introduction to difference. The classroom, I believe, needs to be attentive to the ways in which it *makes room*. bell hooks names this particular kind of classroom grace when she writes, "The teacher who can ask of students, 'what do you need in order to learn,' or 'how can I serve?' brings to the work of educating a spirit that honors the students' will to learn."[10] In this sense, asking students how they are hungry, offering forth a feast, and stepping back from the regulation of gluttony opens up the space of learning and risks the messiness of the newly bruised tomato. This kind of tomato is at odds with learnification in several ways: it rejects the neoliberal model of radical individualism by insisting on the necessary import of community, and it situates learning within a particular context—in a word, it eschews the anonymity and objectivity of *traditional* teaching models.

There is hope to be found in the bruised tomato—a tomato grown and cultivated and consumed in ways yet unimagined. So where does hunger come in? "Sometimes," Zimmerman writes, "it's only when somebody puts food in front of you that you realize you were hungry after all."[11] One of the dangers of academic capitalism is that you begin to believe hunger is normal—it takes a deeply indoctrinated classroom to starve and watch starve. But suppose students knew they were not alone? The bruised tomato, I believe, is one way of reinvigorating these community-building rituals of the classroom—of realizing we are hungry—and making space for unintentional knowledges. To live in hunger "means losing the ability to recognize what it takes to maintain a self, a heart, a life,"[12] but to be moved by one's appetite and to lay claim to its desires is to rejoice in the unregulated gluttony of pedagogy.

More often than not, we learn and teach within institutions where knowledge production is structured to reinforce and replicate the ostensible beauty of an unmarred tomato—a genetically modified pedagogy—but we forget that the tomato is always already coated in fine traces of dirt, the dusty milieu of its specific epistemic citizenship. We cannot scrub knowledge clean of the messy political, and so to embrace the *bruised* tomato is to offer forth a space animated by love, by care labour, and to give value to the solemn splendour of truths never yet imagined.

At the time of writing this, I am still learning every day what it means to inhabit the classroom as a crazy woman, to feel all the time the pressures and prescriptions of the university. "Recognizing our own and our students' embodiment," write Berg and Seeber, "shifts the emphasis of our pedagogy."[13] This piece proffers one way to warrant this hope of Berg and Seeber. The bruised tomato becomes possible when we acknowledge and affirm our appetites: tastes that we long for and perhaps have only begun to feel or experience. Pedagogy need not always be pleasurable, but it must be critical, communal, and, above all, it must make space for myriad and ever-changing embodied interactions. While the tomatoes we encounter, students and teachers alike, will surely never be the same, we can make of them a salad to carry with us, bruises and all, into moments *beyond* the classroom. And so let us eat while we are hungry—feast together on the mutilated pedagogies before us—because we have starved ourselves long enough.

NOTES

1. bell hooks, *Teaching Community: A Pedagogy of Hope* (New York: Routledge, 2003), 86.
2. Maggie Berg and Barbara K. Seeber, *The Slow Professor: Challenging the Culture of Speed in the Academy* (Toronto: University of Toronto Press, 2016), x.
3. Jess Zimmerman, "Hunger Makes Me," *Hazlitt*, July 7, 2016, https://hazlitt.net/feature/hunger-makes-me.
4. Sabrina Scott, *Witchbody* (Chicago: Perfectly Acceptable Press, 2016), n.p.
5. Berg and Seeber, *The Slow Professor*, 17.
6. Sara Ahmed, *Queer Phenomenology: Orientations, Objects, Others* (Durham, NC: Duke University Press, 2006), 9.
7. Lorraine Code, *Ecological Thinking: The Politics of Epistemic Location* (Oxford: Oxford University Press, 2006), 72.
8. Berg and Seeber, *The Slow Professor*, 2.
9. Gert Biesta, *The Beautiful Risk of Education* (New York: Routledge, 2014), 7.
10. hooks, *Teaching Community*, 92.
11. Zimmerman, "Hunger Makes Me."
12. Zimmerman.
13. Berg and Seeber, *The Slow Professor*, 36.

WORKS CITED

Ahmed, Sara. *Queer Phenomenology: Orientations, Objects, Others*. Durham, NC: Duke University Press, 2006.

Berg, Maggie, and Barbara K. Seeber. *The Slow Professor: Challenging the Culture of Speed in the Academy*. Toronto: University of Toronto Press, 2016.

Biesta, Gert. *The Beautiful Risk of Education*. New York: Routledge, 2014.

Code, Lorraine. *Ecological Thinking: The Politics of Epistemic Location*. Oxford: Oxford University Press, 2006.

hooks, bell. *Teaching Community: A Pedagogy of Hope*. New York: Routledge, 2003.

Lorde, Audre. *Sister Outsider: Essays and Speeches*. New York: Crossing, 2007.

Scott, Sabrina. *Witchbody*. Chicago: Perfectly Acceptable Press, 2016.

Zimmerman, Jess. "Hunger Makes Me." *Hazlitt*, July 7, 2016, https://hazlitt.net/feature/hunger-makes-me.

III

The Political

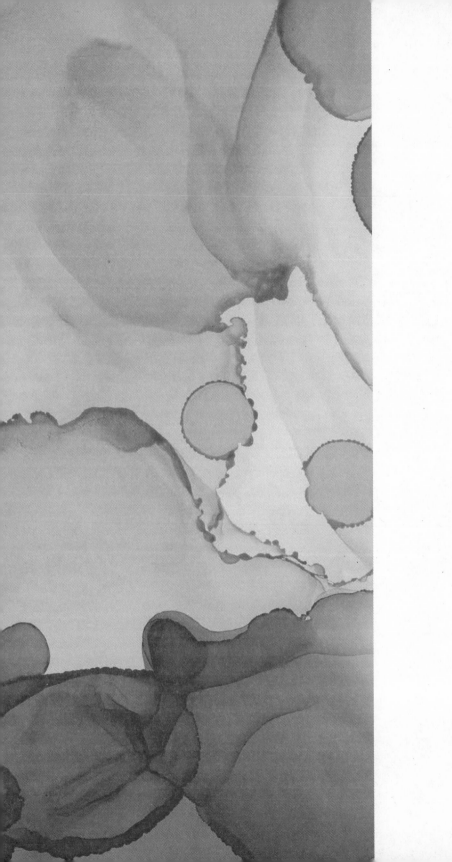

Practising How We
Read What We Read

NAMRATA MITRA

WHAT IS AT STAKE in the first text you assign in an English literature course? A lot: it is the first sequence of the course design and it frames how we read subsequent texts. The frames of reading define the limits of what we as readers register in the plot, context, and character while other details fade into the periphery or outside the frame.[1] Our frames are typically shaped by the interplay between narrative point of view from which the story is being told and our previous text encounters. Consider how the following questions press against the frames of reading a novel. Which characters enter this story without a history? Who drops out of the narrative somewhere along the way? Which lives are framed into focus in the narrative? Which events are explicitly stated and which are suggested? Most significantly, with which character(s) do(es) the narrator seem to share an assumed knowledge about how the world is and how it ought to be, and whose point of view is defined against that "common sense" world view?

This chapter addresses the questions above with the aim of exploring some pedagogical ends, designs, and methods in teaching postcolonial literature in a North American college classroom. It is divided into three sections. In the first section, I situate some literary debates about textual interpretation in the context of my first ever postcolonial literature course. In the second section,

I discuss a literary adaptation project. My students take a section of a post-colonial novel or a short story and adapt it from the point of view of another character. I then draw on Judith Butler to unpack what is at stake in unsettling the frames of our recognition by shifting the narrative point of view. In the third section, I discuss some dissonant reading practices. It is the very activity of reading, I argue, that is at stake in postcolonial classrooms. In fact, learning happens through performed acts of reading.[2]

First Frame: The Classroom

When it was time for me to teach my first undergraduate postcolonial liter-ature course, I settled on Amitav Ghosh's *The Glass Palace*, which I thought clearly framed the dissonance between the violence of colonization and the justifications of the empire. I chose it, in other words, because it showed the "legitimation" of imperial violence—exemplified by the lofty promises of bringing social liberation to the colonies—as the dissembling of colonial practices, rather than as, in fact, legitimate. *The Glass Palace* is a historical novel about the British colonization of Burma (since renamed Myanmar) and the establishment of British India. I did not anticipate, however, an entirely other kind of dissonance that arose within the classroom, a dissonance between my own reading of the novel and that of my students.

The novel begins with the third Anglo–Burmese War in 1885. The British forces win. To avoid civil unrest and possible uprising, the victors decide against killing King Thebaw, his pregnant wife, Queen Supalayat, and their daughter. Instead, the royal family and a small retinue are immediately exiled to British India where they are temporarily placed in Madras. The powerless king "unaccountably" begins exhibiting odd behaviour; he demands vast quantities of pork, which he consumes until sickness.[3] What is "unaccountable" to the narrator may be less mysterious to the reader, who has until then closely followed the king's fall, surrender, and exile. Soon after, we are told that "curious fantasies began to enter the King's mind," and he settles on a new plan: to make the gift of a large gold plate set with a hundred and fifty rubies to his unborn child. The king, secretly, starts selling his few remaining jewels that were "lost" in the hands of the British during their transfer. Mr. Cox, appointed to oversee the royal family in exile, hovers over the deposed king. The Tamil servants are only able to sell the jewels for a fraction of their worth. Mr. Cox's spies ensure he finds out. He immediately reprimands the king, who becomes more secretive in his sales and recovers even less money. Learning of this, Mr. Cox and other British officers acted decisively: "they declared that the King couldn't be trusted with money and enacted a law appropriating his family's most valuable properties."[4]

I read the last line aloud in class, mostly for dramatic effect. Here we had just collectively arrived at the passage of a British law allegedly enacted in the economic interest of the king, yet which ironically passed all of his remaining wealth into the hands of the British. One of my students looked up and said, "Well, I think what Mr. Cox did was right. The king wasn't acting responsibly." Some other heads nodded. It suddenly became obvious that many of the students agreed. I must have looked stunned since they looked at me, puzzled in turn.

I grew up in India, where school history textbooks gloss over British colonization as a period of oppression and represent the formation of the independent nation-state in 1947 as the radical beginning of freedom for Indians, and so the hypocrisy of this colonial law seemed obvious to me. It may have taken me longer to notice the present-day Indian government's colonial exploits in Kashmir or state-sanctioned violence against religious minorities, but I had been trained to quickly identify the wrong of the British colonization. However, my students had grown up in the US, during the decade in which the government had framed the Iraq and Afghanistan invasions as a necessary evil to deliver the gift of political democracy to all and social liberation to women. The history of America as they had learnt in school begins with the arrival of European settlers with very little account of life, culture, and politics prior to colonialization. The story of their nation had always been told from the point of view of colonial settlers, and when the American nationalist movement found itself under British political control, they read a story of a successful War of Independence (1776). This is a different narrative and legacy from the failed Indian "Sepoy Mutiny" (1857) named and narrated from British imperial perspectives and only recently reclaimed as the "First [unsuccessful] War of Independence" in South Asian history.

My primary imperative as a professor of postcolonial studies at that point became to demonstrate the self-interest at work in the supposedly disinterested colonial laws of property appropriation, particularly the imperial investments in modern secular liberalism from which these laws emanate. I reasoned that the aim of my courses should be to render recognizable epistemic violence to an audience mostly taught to recognize only physical violence. However, such a political aim becomes more complicated within the discipline of literature, since the broader questions about *what* constitutes literature and *how* textual meanings are generated are unstable and continually disrupt definitive conclusions about the meaning of a text. A politically committed reading of a text becomes unviable in a literature classroom, since that would amount to declaring the interpretation and outcome of a text even before the class discussion on what we are noticing differently in the text before us and its implications for interpreting the text.

If the same text means many different things to different readers, like it did for some of my students and for me, then on what basis do "we" (the readers situated in specific times and places) provisionally settle debates on what a text means? Should clues from the historical context guide the interpretation of a text? Or should we instead focus on unpacking the assumptions and world views of the specific interpretive community reading the text?[5] An exploration of the historical context of a literary text may not fully explain why my students and I took the same arrangement of words in Ghosh's *The Glass Palace* to mean such different things. A better explanation for our varying understanding of the novel may be that we emerged from different "interpretive communities."[6] As proponents of reader response theory would argue, the readers' historical and literary backgrounds, which form the basis of how they render texts intelligible, become as salient as those of the text to explain why the same text appears to produce divergent meanings to different groups of readers. However, recognizing how *our* past experiences and textual encounters shape our current readings surely cannot be the goal of the unpacking of a postcolonial text, especially if "we" are situated in the imperial headquarters in the West. Would that not be egregious solipsism presented as the study of alterity?[7]

In the context of postcolonial literature courses, surely, understanding the harms of colonization requires situating a text in its historical context. Yet choosing the path of historically contextualized readings hardly settles the debate. After all, the "historical context" of a literary narrative is usually only available to the literature reader as a set of historical narratives in which the literary concerns about the relationship among the reader, text, narrative point of view, and context is differed once more. As literature scholars, we often have to remind ourselves that the discipline of history is also subject to these debates. If a Marxist historical narrative lays claim to suppressed historical truths by narrating a history from below with overlooked historical "evidence," such as pamphlets or songs that circulated among peasant rebels, then a poststructuralist critique of such a narrative seeks to interrogate the historian's own standpoint and speaking subject position in the construction of the historical narrative.

Consider the following critique of Marxist historiography by postcolonial historian Dipesh Chakrabarty.[8] Chakrabarty is particularly concerned with the legacy of historicist frames on Marxist historians. A historicist approach divides the past into specific periods or eras with distinct characteristics, such as medieval and modern, or feudal and capitalist, and then places them in order of increasing advancement. Within such a schema, the stage of secular modernity lies at the end of history as the teleological aim of historical progress. Chakrabarty calls into question the narratives of South Asian Marxist historians who frame religiously inspired peasant rebellions as "pre-modern," as though these political movements should advance to the next stage of modernity when peasants will frame their rebellions in secular terms of class consciousness.[9] It seems that the question of how to construct and read historical discourse echoes some literary debates. The claim that we (here and now) can engage with history (there and then) in a nonpresentist way with the right historical evidence can legitimately be countered by a reader-response-based approach that would demand that the historian interrogate how his world view (here and now) shapes his framing of historical "evidence." Accordingly, if as a postcolonial literature professor, I wish to appeal to "historical context" in the classroom, then either I must continue the same literary debate with the historical narratives or I must willingly suspend our disbelief that historical discourse is untroubled by these deliberations. On some occasions, I have chosen the latter in the strategic interest of continuing close reading the novel during the class period. So what is at stake in how we navigate among these different frames of reading in our classrooms? In the next section, I make a case for engaging with an interplay of frames rather than trying to locate the "right" one.

Literary Adaptation Assignment Project: "My Tomato Is a Frame"

In teaching Ghosh's *The Glass Palace*, I learned that some of my students seemed ambivalent about the wrongs of the British colonization of Burma. After all, they pointed out, had not Queen Supalayat been ruthless in ordering the murders of all other contenders to the throne so her cousin and husband, Thebaw, would be made king? And didn't she yell and throw things at her servants? Surely, she deserved it! And, yes, while waging war to seize another country's wealth is wrong, didn't some good come out of colonization since the people were no longer subject to a despotic queen? While everyone in the classroom seemed to agree that colonial violence is bad, it nevertheless suddenly seemed to sprout so many silver linings, such as claims about social reform and "progress" through colonization (despite very little historical support for them),[10] that they had to be rapidly diffused. These are commonly held myths about colonization in Europe, North America, and in many anglophone school curriculums in South Asia. To shake some of these certainties, I created an assignment that asked students to produce literary adaptations of existing texts. These adaptations encouraged students to dislodge the frames of their reading by adopting different narrative points of view than those they initially encountered within the novels.

The literary adaptation project has three main parts. First, we select a passage from the text, such as the one described in the introduction. We close read the section and pick out phrases and words that offer specific details about the setting, events, and character details. Then, taking those phrases and words, each student group crafts the narrative from the point of view of a different character. They are required to use the same set of selected phrases from the previous close-reading activity and to stick to the same plot points but are encouraged to read them against the grain by fleshing out the narrative between the shared phrases.

Accordingly, the same passage with the same list of specific textual phrases and details can yield very different adaptations. The process of crafting these narratives sometimes forces students to ask questions about the world views and cosmologies of the different characters the text does not include. For instance, the passage described earlier in this chapter can be told as a story in which King Thebaw fearfully and furtively sells his jewels to ensure that he can give his newborn the gift of the last of his jewels from Burma before they too are "lost" under the supervision of the British. In this adaptation, he could be as keenly aware of his own diminishing wealth as Mr. Cox is. Or it can be narrated from the point of view of Mr. Cox, who discovers the king's inability to follow the terms of exile, and then, bristling with the righteousness of fairness afforded by secular liberalism, decides to discipline the king with the formal letter of the law.

Particularly significant are those times when two groups adapt a passage from the point of view of the same character but produce very different stories based on their diverging reader responses. A week later, when I first introduced this activity, two groups decided to adapt a section from Queen Supalayat's narrative perspective. While one group saw her as a deeply wronged queen trying to hang on to the vestiges of her former power, the other group, who had inter-pellated her as a "bitch," drew on the tropes of Disney movies to cast her as a "Wicked Queen" who had suffered a just fall. Both groups had adapted the same passage from the novel and had used the same list of quotations we had picked out during our close-reading class activity for our literary adaptation activity. The story of the two queens in these two adaptations revealed as much about the tastes, biases, and ways of seeing of the readers and authors of the adaptations as it did about the text from which it was adapted. It is in these moments that the reader response theorists' insistence on attending to the cultural context of "interpretive [reading] communities" has the greatest import in the classroom.

As we collaborate on our adaptations, narrating the same colonial encounter in the novel from various vantage points situated in different world views, we dismantle expectations of a singular "truth" of the text. Rather, it is in the interplay of the multiple lenses through which we unpack a text that we learn how different narratives produce the effect of different realities. Since the colonizer's narratives of colonial encounters are most widely circulated and come to be framed as unshakeable facts, the practice of unsettling those ways of reading a text is a fruitful excise in a postcolonial studies classroom. Invariably, toward the end of the semester, unexpected developments emerge: some students, seeking to champion a narrative from the point of view of a subjugated character, become so attached to their version of the story that they want to claim it as the truest account. Surely, they argue, it is the goal of postcolonial studies to tell stories from the point of view of those silenced and forgotten in history textbooks and the current news! However, it is at these very teachable moments that we collectively deliberate on the aims of the (in) discipline of postcolonial literature, and the ways it allows us to interrogate how some narrative patterns and points of view come to be regarded as more "reliable" than others. That is, the aim of literary adaptation, as a long-standing genre, is decidedly not to "find" the "authentic view" or to locate the "truest meaning" of a literary text but rather to unmoor such attachments of certainty to truths produced by narratives. Such a desire for epistemic certainty in telling the definitive version of history from below has not been entirely absent from the history of postcolonial studies.[11] Instead, the process of literary adaptation in a literature course ought to maintain a critical space of uncertainty that does not foreclose future possible meanings rendered by the different animations of the text.

Judith Butler's *Frames of War: When Is Life Grievable?* provides a robust theoretical account of why such uncertainty is valuable. Butler's account prompted me initially to develop the adaptation assignment, and now, after teaching and reflecting on the assignment, its emphasis on the interplay of different frames of reality reinforces my sense that postcolonial teaching should solicit uncertainty, rather than the kind of certainty that emerges from definitive accounts of history from below.

The *framing* of an event of war, particularly an imperial war, shapes how "we," the viewers who are located in relative safety, recognize its import: the framing solicits its recognizability as loss, as insignificant, or as necessary and even desirable. Our "perceptible field of reality" renders suffering visible or invisible and shapes how we respond to it.[12] Each frame invites the viewer's participation in adopting and reproducing the frames of seeing. The relation between the framing of a scene of war and the responses it tends to elicit is well understood by the state, and it guides how it describes its own violence. The people on whom bombs are dropped, for example, are not soft-fleshed bodies vulnerable to being torn and bled by bombs and bullets but rather are "targets" and "collateral damage." The existence of "enemy combatants" is a threat, and the removal of a "target" is an accomplishment, not a grievable loss of life. Accordingly, there is a major shift in the affective response, a shift from grieving the loss of another person to the sense of indifference or accomplishment in response to these deaths.

What is at the centre of the frame? What lies at the edges? What possible scenes of war lie outside the frame, scenes that keep threatening to peep through and undo the contained scene of war? Here lies the liberatory potential: if the frames of an image mark the limits of what we apprehend, recognize as real, and shape how we respond to it, then the unsteady liminal space in between shifting frames or multiple iterations of nearly the same frame can disrupt our epistemic certainty in what we take as unshakably real. Butler writes the following:

> As frames break from themselves in order to install themselves, other possibilities for apprehension emerge. When those frames that govern the relative and differential recognizability of lives come apart—as part of the very mechanism of their circulation— it becomes possible to apprehend something about what or who is living but has not been generally "recognized" as a life.[13]

New apprehensions of life and loss are possible because the frames shift and replace each other, not because a potentially all-inclusive frame emerged. The same holds for loss and harm rendered recognizable in narratives of domination. Multiple literary adaptations of the same text can generate play among different frames, and each can show what another erases or ignores. On the other hand, the desire to treat a singular literary or historical narrative, written from the point of view of marginalized characters, as the "truest" historical account tends to be based on the hope that there is an all-encompassing, universal frame that exists and that it is just a question of finding its location and finally establishing it as the most commonly reproduced one in history textbooks and in the media. My students who become strongly attached to one literary adaptation over all others, claiming that it is the most faithful postcolonial account of what "really" happened, often tend to think that their search for the fairest and most universal frame has finally borne promise.

However, while they are not alone or new in their desire for certainty in the historical record, there is a need to foster skepticism in reading literary and historical narratives alike.

We all deploy frames when we teach. My own teaching, moreover, is increasingly invested in soliciting attention *to* frames. Indeed, perhaps the best way to sum up my teaching through literary adaptation is to say, "my tomato is a frame." This metaphor for teaching practices—the tomato—is one to which several contributors to this collection subscribe, and it stems from a passage in Zadie Smith's *On Beauty*.[14] In it, Vee, an undergraduate student, and her friends insightfully dub their college course offerings not based on their official titles but based on what they assess is the guiding theme and limits of the course in relation to "tomatoes." As she explains the concept of the tomato to the now-sighing art professor, Howard, Vee points out, "Your class is all about never ever saying I like the *tomato*...The tomato is just totally revealed as this phoney construction that can't lead you to some higher truth—nobody is pretending that the tomato will save your life."[15] Howard's tomato is focused on dismantling why and how artworks come to be valued as beautiful. So much so that "one of the worst things" that could be said in his class is that one actually likes a work of art. In sharp contrast, Vee's father, also an art professor in the same institution, has quite the opposite tomato: he teaches that the "Tomato saves."[16] Ada Jaarsma and I have mused about the dynamics of tomatoes in the classroom for several years. We have speculated, for example, that professors and students are likely to have different reads on a given professor's tomato. This has not stopped us, however, from trying to identify our own tomatoes. While my tomato admittedly changes based on the discipline in which I teach, I have concluded that, in literature classrooms, my tomato must be a frame. And I borrow this locution from Butler. I begin every course with a short stack of novels, some poems, plays, and literary theory essays. Then my students and I navigate each world in each text by asking about the narrative point of view through which images are made visible and arguments intelligible, and we explore how changes in vantage points can produce a very different effect of images and arguments.

Tomato-Picking Season in the English Literary Greenhouse

So what do literary tomatoes look like? In my second year of teaching English literature at my current institution, I was assigned to teach "English 314: Introduction to Literary Studies," the aim of which is to introduce students to the discipline—or rather its lack—in English literature. In this course, we read literary theorists arguing about what constitutes literature, how to interpret texts, and the function of literature itself. But here is a challenge at the heart of teaching literature: it is basically always tomato-picking season in the English literary greenhouse. For example, literature professors will likely take a stance in relation to arguments for or against the canon, and their commitments to subtend, revise, or demolish it will determine which "tomatoes" are deemed nutritious and important to include on syllabi. Tomatoes, in this case, help shape the curriculum of a given course, a curriculum that will likely be in tension with those who teach down the hall. In addition, "tomatoes" also emerge out of disciplinary arguments about how best to interpret literary texts: Is one's own context as a reader the most salient ingredient of interpretation, or is it the context of the literary text itself? In this case, tomatoes in the form of disciplinary presumptions help shape the activities and orientations of assignments within a course. Since my own tomato is a "frame," I ask my students to pick, taste, and share dissonant tomatoes in order to draw out the tensions between them. As I explain, my tomato is a tomato that opens up, rather than adjudicates or closes down, questions about interpretation.

Becoming skeptical readers of fiction can be unsettling for students whose primary interest in literature has been nurtured through vicarious pleasure and identification with the protagonists of novels. This is commonly manifest in student comments about the relatability of a text, which is then used as grounds to adjudicate on the merits of the text. This can be frustrating for professors such as myself because texts situated in other communities and unfamiliar contexts are sometimes rejected because of their seeming "weirdness." While it may seem that the cultivation of skeptical reading practices is akin to Vee's assessment of Howard's tomato, which forbids liking the tomato, that is not the case here since I do also ask them how they "felt" reading a text. There is a major difference between his tomato and the one in the postcolonial literature class at our small liberal arts college. Asking and exploring why students like, love, hate, or are disturbed by how a text is helpful in recognizing how we as readers are implicated in the narratives and the world views that we encounter in postcolonial literature. If I and some others in class cannot recognize King Thebaw's grief, that does not mean that it does not exist but that *we* cannot recognize it because the norms of the recognizability of grief by which our understanding has been shaped exclude the representation of the grief that lies before us. To recognize that there are limits to our frames of reading is not the end but rather a necessary starting point to apprehend alterity.

Conclusion

Arguments about the location of "the tomato" (here and now, situated in the reading communities, or there and then, in the historical and geographical contexts of the literary work) should shift based on the context of its emergence. Teaching postcolonial literature in North America has often required that I insist that the tomato is not about us or who is relatable to us. However, after an entirely different experience of teaching peasants in 1950s Brazil, Paulo Freire argued against the "banking concept of education," which assumed the teachers know everything, the students know nothing, and it is the teacher's task to deposit knowledge in the students.[17] His critique is aimed at demonstrating how educational institutions often perpetuate the hierarchies of the status quo. When students from marginalized communities walk into a university classroom, their world views and histories are absent in the dominant forms of knowledge. Typically, marginalized students reading "The Great Books" in the humanities disciplines do not have the privilege to express interest in a text or reject it on grounds of its "relatability," since most of the texts in this tradition place those groups into the distant background of the narrative frame, if not outside of it altogether. In such cases, I would argue that there is an urgent need for a tomato contrary to mine: one that focuses on the students and their knowledge of the world. Here the tomato is decidedly you, the student. Here I am echoing Peter Felton, who argues that good teaching must be "grounded" in the local cultural and scholarly context. Moreover, the social, political, and cultural context must speak to the shaping of curriculum and teaching practices.[18] In a similar vein, bell hooks draws on Freire when she recounts her experiences soon after the racial integration of schools in the American South. Unlike her old classes taught by black teachers and designed for black students, the new ones were not spaces that fostered "excitement" in radical pedagogy. Instead, the excitement of black students was considered a dangerous thing in integrated schools managed by white teachers and administrators. She quickly discovered the underlying tomato shared across the curriculum in school and college: "to learn obedience to authority."[19] As a mode of resistance, she argues in favour of fostering excitement as the predominant affect in teaching and learning. Taking the cue from hooks, I would like to return to the humanities greenhouse and think about how to cross-pollinate and nurture a range of exciting tomatoes that change and grow differently with different students. I offer my own tomato in this chapter—"My Tomato Is a Frame"—as one tomato among countless others in order to invite readers to encounter the significance of dissonant tomatoes.

NOTES

1. Judith Butler, *Frames of War: When Is Life Grievable?* (New York: Verso, 2010).
2. For more on acts of learning, such as "think alouds" in framing philosophical questions, see Stephen Bloch-Schulman, "A Critique of Methods in the Scholarship of Teaching and Learning in Philosophy," *Teaching & Learning Inquiry* 4.1 (March 2016).
3. Amitav Ghosh, *The Glass Palace* (New York: Random House, 2002), 45.
4. Ghosh, 46.
5. Stanley Fish, *Is There a Text in this Class? The Authority of Interpretive Communities* (Cambridge, MA: Harvard University Press, 2000).
6. Fish.
7. See Gert Biesta's critique of a constructivist approach to teaching, which is built on the Socratic assumption that students are already repositories of knowledge, and it is the task of the teacher to assist them in accessing that knowledge through class activities in "Receiving the Gift of Teaching: From 'Learning From' to 'Being Taught By,'" *Studies in Philosophical Education* 32 (2013): 451.
8. See Dipesh Chakrabarty's interrogation of the narrative subject position of the historian in *Provincializing Europe: Postcolonial Thought and Historical Difference* (Princeton: Princeton University Press, 2000).
9. Chakrabarty, 97–115.
10. While the British commonly legitimized their colonization of India in terms of social reform, specifically women's liberation, Ghosh, in a letter to Dipesh Chakrabarty, argues the British did not even try to appeal to this justification when colonizing Burma, since it had a record of equal status accorded to men and women of the like not seen or practised in England. See "A Correspondence on Provincializing Europe," *Radical History* 83 (Spring 2002): 157.
11. The aim of telling history from below or "the history of the people" was the chief aim of early Subaltern Studies history, which began in South Asia in the 1980s. See Ranajit Guha, introduction to *A Subaltern Studies Reader: 1986–1995* (New Delhi: Oxford University Press, 2007).
12. See Butler, *Frames of War*, 64.
13. Butler, 64.
14. See Ada Jaarsma's discussion of pedagogical tomatoes in "Design, Disability, and Play: The Animal Politics of Education," *Gender and Education* 28.2 (2016): 199.
15. Zadie Smith, *On Beauty* (New York: Penguin, 2005), 312.
16. Smith, 313.

17. Paolo Freire, *Pedagogy of the Oppressed* (New York: Bloomsbury, 2000).
18. Peter Felton, "Principles of Good Practice in SoTL," *Teaching & Learning Inquiry* 1.1 (2013).
19. bell hooks, *Teaching to Transgress: Education as a Practice of Freedom* (New York: Routledge, 1994), 4.

WORKS CITED

Biesta, Gert. "Receiving the Gift of Teaching: From 'Learning From' to 'Being Taught By.'" *Studies in Philosophical Education* 32 (2013): 449–61.

Bloch-Schulman, Stephen. "A Critique of Methods in the Scholarship of Teaching and Learning in Philosophy." *Teaching & Learning Inquiry* 4.1 (March 2016): 1–15.

Butler, Judith. *Frames of War: When Is Life Grievable?* New York: Verso, 2010.

Chakrabarty, Dipesh. *Provincializing Europe: Postcolonial Thought and Historical Difference*. Princeton: Princeton University Press, 2000.

Felton, Peter. "Principles of Good Practice in SoTL." *Teaching & Learning Inquiry* 1.1 (2013): 121–25.

Fish, Stanley. *Is There a Text in this Class? The Authority of Interpretive Communities*. Cambridge, MA: Harvard University Press, 2000.

Freire, Paolo. *Pedagogy of the Oppressed*. New York: Bloomsbury, 2000.

Ghosh, Amitav. *The Glass Palace*. New York: Random House, 2002.

Ghosh, Amitav, and Dipesh Chakrabarty. "A Correspondence on Provincializing Europe." *Radical History* 83 (Spring 2002): 146–72.

Guha, Ranajit. Introduction to *A Subaltern Studies Reader: 1986–1995*, ix–xxii. New Delhi: Oxford University Press, 2007.

hooks, bell. *Teaching to Transgress: Education as a Practice of Freedom*. New York: Routledge, 1994.

Jaarsma, Ada S. "Design, Disability, and Play: The Animal Politics of Education." *Gender and Education* 28.2 (2016): 195–212.

Smith, Zadie. *On Beauty*. New York: Penguin, 2005.

Dissonance, Resistance, and Perspectival Pedagogies

RACHEL JONES

> The emphasis on safety in feminist settings often served as a barrier to cross-racial solidarity because these encounters did not feel "safe" and were often charged with tension and conflict... Trusting our ability to cope in situations where racialized conflict arises is far more fruitful than insisting on safety as always the best or only basis for bonding.
>
> —bell hooks, *Teaching Community*

> Not every "how" of teaching practices proffers the same degree of playful enthusiasms... When play fails, Massumi explains, it gives way to the pull of the given, and we find ourselves swayed by the back-pull of established necessity... When play fails, despair upholds the seemingly obligatory norms that constitute the given.
>
> —Ada S. Jaarsma, *Kierkegaard after the Genome*

Pedagogical Dissonance

The starting point for this reflection on teaching is an experience of dissonance. Not the risky yet potentially fruitful dissonance that hooks invokes above, and instead, the tension between exactly that kind of pedagogically generative dissonance and the "back-pull of established necessity" (to borrow from Jaarsma) that can sometimes be the response. For those of us who teach in part to cultivate an unlearning of racism (or homophobia, transphobia, sexism, ableism: colonizing logics of all kinds), in ourselves as well as our students,[1] one of the risks is that such deliberately unsettling teaching can often (perhaps unavoidably) provoke a defensive reaction.[2]

I am thinking of the kind of moment Jaarsma describes, when the cognitive dissonance produced by troubling the established but often invisible value of whiteness results not in transformation but the reactive pushback of anger, denial, or withdrawal.[3] Such "back-pull" manifests in class discussions when a student suggests that white folks are now the victims of racist oppression because of the "unfair" assumption that they are all racist; or when someone insists that, the complexities of intersex and social gender norms notwithstanding, your gender is really decided by "what you have between your legs."[4] Citing the words in this decontextualized way captures some of their visceral, interruptive force, but misses much of what matters in the moment: their tone, register, and accompanying body language; the already existing dynamics between who speaks and who is silent; the way those words cut into the mix of bodies in the classroom.

The response to such comments is often another series of reactions—bodily, affective, sometimes discursive: from raised eyebrows and frustrated sighs ("really? again?") to relieved nodding of heads ("thank goodness someone said that"); embarrassed glances or a determined staring at the floor; a collective intake of breath or audible expressions of dissent (or assent). Often they produce a temporary block in the discussion in the form of a sudden, discomforted silence: a charged moment where it seems sides might be taken and the process of thinking together falters.

Learning to live with that silence and helping to make it a space where thinking continues to happen is one of the familiar challenges of teaching, along with learning how to speak into that silence (and, crucially, when not to) and how to encourage others to inhabit it as a site of possibility because of (rather than despite) its discomfort. hooks's words about the need for such risky encounters in the classroom resonate even more strongly in the context of the contemporary US, where Donald Trump's presidency has exacerbated deeply rooted racialized tensions and lent false legitimacy to racist, misogynist, ableist, homophobic, and transphobic attitudes and their accompanying violences. In this context, the urgency of "unlearning racism"[5] has only intensified, as has the need for "safe spaces" that offer respite from hateful and exclusionary grammars of existence.

Yet, as hooks notes, there is an implicit tension between these needs: the emphasis on safety can push against the risky, conflict-riven work involved in exposing complicity and confronting the unjust social and political relations that subtend white privilege. To navigate this tension, it seems crucial to avoid a false opposition between critical pedagogy and "safe spaces." The latter can take many forms, and while *all* spaces should be free of racialized or sexualized violence (including hate speech), there is also a need for places where those most likely to be subjected to such violence are free from the need to defend themselves from more quotidian assaults on their existence—those woven into everyday words, gestures, and glances—as well as from the exhausting labour of having to continually explain and educate. At the same time, however, if we wish to mobilize a dissonant pedagogy in the name of social justice, then we also need to cultivate spaces where it is *safe to enter into* more fraught and unsettling discussions. Such spaces depend among other things on a fostering of trust, to allow discomforting tensions to be inhabited and explored from irreducibly different starting points.

In her 2016 book *Inclinations*, Adriana Cavarero suggests that our human, natal existence is characterized by the vulnerability that makes relations possible.[6] Erinn Gilson's work adds to this picture, showing how epistemic vulnerability is a necessary condition of undoing structural ignorance,[7] the kind of ignorance that subtends racist social relations, as Charles Mills and Linda Martin Alcoff have compellingly argued.[8] If this is so, then the difficult work of unlearning racism will need to attend to the existential and ontological vulnerability that makes all pedagogical relations possible, and to cultivate the epistemic vulnerability that makes it possible to challenge existing conditions of privilege and oppression. And, again, while these joint aims might seem in tension (cultivating epistemic vulnerability might seem likely to heighten existential vulnerability), they are, in fact, necessarily coupled. Unless we recognize (in ourselves before others) the *existential* unease that goes along with having one's own complicit ignorance exposed, and develop ways of working through such exposure, we are unlikely to cultivate the *epistemic* vulnerability that allows us to unlearn together and that holds open the possibility for change.

Nonetheless, as both Cavarero and Judith Butler discuss,[9] "we" are not all situated in the same way when it comes to vulnerability, or, of course, racism. The shared vulnerability of a constitutively relational existence is routinely exploited by an inherently racializing capitalism[10] to produce a differential (and profoundly unjust) distribution of social and political conditions of precarity. If it is not to replicate or exacerbate such injustice, the kind of dissonant pedagogy that some of us strive toward should not come at the expense of those already made most precarious by the very structures of entrenched oppression and privilege that we seek to dislodge.

This brings me to one of the concerns of this chapter. As someone who has been inspired, partly by hooks, to embrace the transformative potential of dissonance in the classroom, and who to some extent sets out to cultivate dissonance as a way to expose "established necessity" to question, I have found myself increasingly troubled by who might be bearing the affective burden of such a pedagogical approach—and, thus, bearing the affective burden of my desire as a teacher for a transformative pedagogy. At the same time, I am also aware of the danger that, when faced with the "back–pull" that Jaarsma describes, it can be tempting to seek to protect those we perceive to be harmed not only by making it clear that racist, sexist, or homophobic comments are unacceptable, but by resorting to a more moralizing pedagogy, one that sets out to teach others *what* (not) to think rather than how to think differently.

One way of capturing this might be to borrow from de Beauvoir's figure of "the serious man":[11] the one who seeks to deny responsibility by asserting a particular set of values, truths, or norms as unquestionable. The temptation is to respond to the "back–pull" of seriousness with seriousness, closing down the *serious play* that unsettles established certainties and exposes prejudice and privilege to questioning. A dissonance that is simultaneously cognitive, affective, and somatic can be one of many possible effects of such play. My concerns here, then, are twofold: how to engage in the serious play of a dissonant pedagogy without imposing an undue burden on those already most harmed by "the seemingly obligatory norms that constitute the given"; and how to avoid resorting to a moralizing seriousness in response to the reactive and harmful reassertion of those norms and the privileges they confer.

Suffering Dissonance

The view that education involves cultivating moments of dissonance so as to unsettle established ideas has a long philosophical history, as suggested by Arendt's description of Socrates:

> Hence, Socrates, gadfly, midwife, electric ray, is not a philosopher (he teaches nothing and has nothing to teach) and he is not a sophist, for he does not claim to make men wise. He only points out to them that they are not wise, that nobody is…And while he defends himself vigorously against the charge of corrupting the young, he nowhere pretends that he is improving them. Nevertheless, he claims that the appearance in Athens of think– ing and examining represented in himself was the greatest good that ever befell the City…thinking inevitably has a destructive,

undermining effect on all established criteria, values, measurements
of good and evil, in short, on those customs and rules of conduct we
treat of in morals and ethics.[12]

This is not the Socrates of the Allegory of the Cave, leading the uninitiated
forcefully toward transcendent truth, but a Socrates who engages in serious
play, unsettling that which his interlocutors take to be given by leading them
into *aporia*: those moments "without passage" when habitual thinking can
carry us no further. Such moments are not unlike the temporary blockages
to class discussion produced by the "back-pull" of established norms and,
following Jaarsma (who is here drawing on Kierkegaard), both might be
described in terms of despair. The difference is that, in the first case, Socratic
aporia confounds habitual thinking to open a space for the as-yet-unthought,
whereas in the latter the attempt to disrupt existing habits is met with a form
of counter-resistance, an "all-too-unplayful" falling back into seriousness that
threatens to shut down possibilities for thinking otherwise.[13]

As hooks reminds us, pedagogical dissonance is always risky: it
disturbs and disrupts the seemingly given and reroutes thinking and affects
in unpredictable ways. Its unsettling effects can be felt not just as cognitive
disturbance but somatic tension and existential threat. Reactive resistance
might thus be read not as a sign of failure but as indexing the way the class is
touching on precisely the kinds of recalcitrant norms that stand most in need
of questioning. We might then see "back-pull" as part of the "success" of a
dissonant pedagogy. Perhaps such a practice demands a kind of "despair work,"
involving both the exposure of operations of despair—understood as the desire
to re-entrench seemingly established norms as unquestionable—and a collective
working through of their implications.

Certainly, such moments often lead those of us who teach to despair,
making us question our methods or our ability to connect with our students.
When we encounter pushback against a curriculum that we were hoping would
unsettle the given, we are reminded not only that students do not always enjoy
our classes[14] but that they do not necessarily feel caught up in the shared critical
project we had hoped to inspire. Perhaps even more obviously, the student who
speaks back against the troubling of dominant norms is also affectively moved:
disturbed by what has been read or said, sometimes agitated, perhaps angry.
Others express discomfort via withdrawal, a refusal to participate or even to
attend. A critical pedagogy that seeks to mobilize dissonance for change needs
to avoid such moments of discomfort turning into occasions for shaming and
blaming; there need to be ways back for those who trap themselves into corners

or whose comments might be found offensive by others—the possibility
of revising one's position needs to remain open, as do ways back into the
collaborative exercise of thinking together, even when one's views might have
jeopardized that very process. There is no clear-cut line between exposing
unquestioned attachments to oppressive gender norms in ways that can be
worked with, and producing a reactive defensiveness that only tends to
re-entrench. Living with this indeterminacy is one of the demands of a
dissonant pedagogy.

Nonetheless, in the encounter between a teacher and a student who
voices a reactive counter-resistance, it is at least possible for a dialectical,
dialogical work to unfold that allows both to find ways forward, to think
further, to continue working together. The nonlinear temporality of learning also means that what might initially be expressed as defensiveness can
be the sign of a shift still to come. What has begun to trouble me more is
whether, in these moments of re-entrenchment when "established necessities"
are reasserted as unquestionably given, it is those who *already* suffer most
from their effects who are asked to bear the affective burden of a dissonant
pedagogy.[15]

When existing lines of white privilege, or heteronormativity, or
ableism, are re-enforced in the classroom, those for whom these structures
and norms are most harmful, and who are already caught up in the daily
struggle to survive and resist them, can find themselves once again subjected
to them and interpolated *by* them: caught between taking up the burden of
response or saying nothing, between becoming further trapped by an identity
and a speaking position thrust upon them—one that tends to reduce the
speaker to the status of "native informant"[16]—or refusing such capture via
a silence that can easily be felt as complicity or (self-)betrayal. In this way,
reactive "back-pull" reanimates the double bind of oppression,[17] as well as
repeating an already socially entrenched harm. It is the very terms of this
oppressive "either/or" that need to be refused, through the resistant strategies
of those well used to encountering it as well as the interventions of allies.
Nonetheless, my concern here is with the way that a dissonant pedagogy can
(at times) reimpose both the original harm and the burden of refusal on those
for whom it seeks justice.

Such problems are compounded by the asymmetry that means that those
whose position of privilege or alignment with entrenched norms is questioned
will typically find that privilege (or those norms) reaffirmed when they leave the
classroom. For this reason, we need to be wary of the neoliberal appropriation
that reduces dissonance to a pedagogical tool that can be calibrated to produce

just the right amount and kind of discomfort to benefit the individual learner. Here dissonance is mobilized to increase self-esteem, improve capacities for managing social relations, or cultivate resilience in ways that are supposed to help students in the "enterprise" of leading their lives to success.[18] On this thoroughly individualized, depoliticized approach, there is no way to attend to the asymmetrical social structures that a critical pedagogy might seek to interrogate: no way to distinguish, *as different in kind*, the psychological discomfort produced when white privilege is called into question, and the reinstitution of oppression that occurs when racist or homophobic views are reinserted as unquestionable necessities.

Being asked to give something up that has given one an unfair social advantage, while it may be painful and even threatening to one's existing identity, does not diminish one's possibilities for meaningful existence so much as *increase* the possibility of giving one's existence meaning (rather than allowing its meaning to be determined by already existing injustices). In contrast, for those already oppressed by existing social norms and structures, and whose possibilities for giving existence meaning are thereby constrained, if not annulled,[19] the reassertion of those norms within the classroom not only constitutes the repetition of a harm, it also closes down a space in which those existential possibilities might be (at least partially) reclaimed.

The possibility of mitigating such harm is complicated by the fact that, in the classroom situation, it is often impossible to know in any clear-cut way who might be being most harmed, or how. This might seem to be more the case with homophobic, transphobic, or ableist comments than the anti-black racism grounded in the "epidermal racial schema"[20] that governs the post-Enlightenment West and North and that ties race (and racism) to the visible marker of skin colour. Yet this racializing schema not only produces black bodies as hypervisible in ways that can reinforce a tendency to call on students of colour and expect them to take on the burden of responding to racism; it can also lead to assumptions about harm that presume affective homogeneity and that can overwrite those students' more complex, knowing, unsurprised, resistant, and (most of all) divergent responses. Such assumptions fill in a space that would be better left open-ended and uncertain. Thus, rather than seeking to clear away the uncertainty that can accompany the moment of reactive "back-pull" in terms of who it most harms and how, I would suggest that this is another of the contingencies that a dissonant pedagogy needs to live and work with. The "will to know" who is most harmed (and how) itself does harm, turning subjects of suffering into objects of judgment, and adding the imperative to appear and perform "harmed" to the original damage done.

Despite the reach of biopower and the racializing logics of hypervisibility, what Édouard Glissant calls the "right to opacity"[21] has not yet been entirely eroded. The educational context is one of many places where such opacity needs to be defended.

Of course, much of what happens in these moments of reactive caesura depends on work already done: the degree of trust established, the patterns of speaking and silence formed, the habits of listening cultivated. We can attend with deliberate care to the ways in which both classrooms and curriculums can make space for those typically excluded or silenced by dominant norms. In what we might think of as the little historical a priori[22] of the classroom, the conditions of possibility for engagement have to be reinvented each and every time.

And yet: the pedagogical encounter remains always unpredictable, in terms of directions taken and lines of thinking opened up (or closed down), and opaque, in terms of the range of its effects, both in the moment and across its multiple afterlives. And given this necessary (and welcome) opacity and unpredictability, my questions remain about a pedagogy that deliberately sets out, among other things, to cultivate moments of dissonance, and, in particular, about what happens when such moments meet with the reactive counter-resistance that is, in a sense, a sign of their "success." Who bears the affective weight of such moments? And if the "unlearning" of some (those who have benefitted—whether they want to or not—from unjust social arrangements) depends on an undue affective burden placed on others (those whose positions as subjects are already contested, unstable, or refused), to what extent might these moments function as a repetition of structural injustice rather than its displacement?

In other words, I have begun to wonder whether the deliberate cultivation of risky dissonance in the classroom might itself—at least at times—be a privileged operation: a work of unsettling whose transformative effects are most productive for those who already benefit from social, economic, and political privilege, including in some cases teachers themselves, and that—again, at least at times—depends on the continued oppression and affective labour of others. To what extent is my *own* valuing of dissonance an expression of privilege lent to me by racist, postcolonial, and ableist structures, of whose anchoring power I am often unaware (perhaps in part *because of* my self-identification as a woman in a male-dominated discipline, such that focusing on the ways I am disadvantaged in some structures screens out the ways I am privileged in others)?

To state the obvious: something different is going on when I, as a white feminist (albeit a white anti-racist feminist) cultivate the pedagogical potential of dissonance for the unlearning of racism, and when hooks (as a self-identified black feminist) engages in a similar practice. While I share in the white privilege that is (hopefully) being unsettled, I do not suffer from racist oppression, and this inevitably effects the distribution of affective labour in my classes. As we are reminded by hooks, as well as others who assess the constitutive effects of both standpoint and ignorance,[23] attending to our own differential position (and privilege) as instructors needs to be part of our critical practice if we are to work with the potential of dissonance to effect change without reproducing structural injustice. Rather than a generalizable practice, we need to resituate dissonance within a distributed play of gazes, voices, bodies, and silences, in *non*generalizable ways.

From Moralizing Lessons to Perspectival Pedagogies

As noted above, one possible response to the "back-pull of established necessity" is to turn the risky openness of critical pedagogy into the closure of a moralizing lesson (responding to seriousness with seriousness). I am thinking here not so much of directly and deliberately racist/sexist interventions, to which one can respond just as directly and deliberately, but of the kinds of comments that harbour and perpetuate anti-black, misogynist, homo- or transphobic views, allowing them to recirculate in more or less unknowing ways, and where this constitutive "un-knowing" is part of what needs to be interrogated. I am thinking of those slightly panicked moments, particularly toward the end of a class, when I am unsure how to pull us back from this kind of harm—a harm I feel partly responsible for, insofar as my curriculum design has opened us up to it. In those moments, it can be tempting simply to tell the class what is wrong with a particular viewpoint, rather than showing what can be learnt by staying with the uncomfortable and interrogating it together; to teach *what* to think, rather than undertaking the more time-consuming work required to open up ways of thinking differently.

As Ira Shor notes in an interview with Sheila Macrine, "No pedagogy is neutral, no learning process is value free, no curriculum avoids ideology and power relations... Every educator, then, orients students toward certain values, actions, and language with implications for the kind of society and people these behaviors will produce."[24] If education typically functions "to reproduce the order of society" (as Sylvia Wynter reminds us), it can also be reoriented toward the transformation of "behaviours and attitudes"[25] and the transvaluation of values. Nonetheless, in responding to reactive "back-pull," and in my desire to mitigate harm, I hear my voice becoming moralizing and "schoolmarmish,"[26] in ways that turn an ethical orientation into an increasingly prescriptive set of values and close down possibilities for further discussion. Lynne Huffer helpfully contrasts such "moral policing" with the fostering of disagreement as "the place where politics starts...disagreement happens precisely in those times and places *where divergent positions converge*: in Rancière's terms, convergence in a common world (without a consensus) is the beginning of the *contestation* that not only makes politics possible but also differentiates politics from policing."[27] Huffer's desire to pursue the fissures that "make politics as disagreement possible"[28] is consonant with a critical pedagogy that seeks—among other things—to foster dissonance, the fissures in frames that have the potential to shift established norms.

This valuing of contestation again needs to be distinguished from its (neo) liberal, individualist counterpart, where the value of disagreement is premised on the view that all opinions must be equally heard in the free marketplace of ideas. This particularly pernicious version of the "view from nowhere"[29] embraces disagreement only despairingly or in bad faith, by assuming that it is possible to take up an imaginary position outside the fray, weighing up each of the ideas on offer from some ideally neutral, disembodied, nonimplicated standpoint. To position racist, sexist, homo- or transphobic viewpoints as alternative opinions that "we" can simply "disagree" over is itself a sign of privilege. It assumes not only that we stand outside such viewpoints but that they stand outside of us, in denial of the ways that such toxic ideas invade particular bodies to produce zones of abjection and nonbeing. This deathly logic, like the ideology of the "free market" with which it is more than metaphorically twinned, relies on a sustained forgetting of the material conditions of the production of ideas, as well as their bodily effects.

On Huffer's approach, by contrast, disagreement emerges "*where divergent positions converge*," in a "common world without a consensus." There is no standing above the fray, making supposedly impartial judgments, and, rather, the minimum condition for contestation is not only positionality or situatedness but divergence *between* positions in a world where consensus is not assumed. To allow our own values to be subject to contestation means neither that we have to accept the terms on which they are contested (this is one of the things in contestation) nor that "every worldview...is [to be] abided."[30] If we wish to "orient students to map the world and their relation to it"[31] in ways that are *re*oriented toward social justice, then we need to be able to articulate why and how particular values come to matter and how others do harm. To avoid such articulations settling into new versions of moral self-certainty, we might take a further note from Huffer, whose anti-racist ethics of alterity depend on "an ethical, self-transformative, self-undoing labor that exposes the Cartesian 'I' to its own limits as a rational moral subject."[32]

This "rift-restoring" work of dissonance depends on an ethical orientation that Huffer calls *eros*: "a mode of living both expressed and unexpressed, both appearing and not: an uncertain, embodied, disruptive encounter of subjects with others."[33] In this passage, Huffer provides another figure for the classroom shaped by the divergent perspectives of a dissonant pedagogy, where we need to live with *not*-knowing (the inapparent and unexpressed), as well as with the unsettling of what we thought we knew, if we are to avoid the ethical violence of refusing opacity. Such opacity marks the ways in which we are always "unknown to ourselves, we knowers,"[34] denying any of us the position of moral authority. It also allows the irreducible alterity that marks each of us in relation to others to evade capture, in ways that are necessary to both resistance and survival (to the survival that *is* resistance) for those who are interpolated as the abjected others of dominant norms.

Huffer's suspicions of the moralizing tendency are succinctly expressed in a passage she cites from Foucault: "The search for a form of morality acceptable to everybody in the sense that everyone should submit to it, strikes me as catastrophic."[35] Such catastrophes threaten in part because of what Claudia Rankine and Beth Loffreda describe as the seductive "language of scandal": "We're all a little relieved by scandal. It's so satisfying, so clear, so easy. The wronged. The evildoers. The undeserving…The righteous side taking, the head shaking." The "relieving distraction" of scandal exerts a "heavy gravitational pull,"[36] a counterweight to the "back-pull of established necessity" found in the comforting anchor of moral certainties and clear-cut oppositions. As Saidiya Hartman and Katherine McKittrick show, in texts that are invaluable models of anti-racist pedagogy, the rehearsal of the scandalous becomes one of the ways in which the attempt to critique racialized-sexualized violence can itself repeat that violence.[37] This too can become a moment where the attempt to confront racial injustice in the classroom places an unjust burden on those who already live with its everyday force.

One thing that has become clear to me then is that, as I am not ready to give up on the potentialities of a dissonant pedagogy just yet, I (as a white, anti-racist feminist) need to do more to avoid such repetitions of injustice within the classroom. Cultivating the trust that allows us to enter into contestation with one another while not assuming we all think or feel alike seems crucial here, as does a deliberate de-centring of privileged perspectives to make space for the voices of those accustomed to living with the effects of structural injustice, as feminist standpoint theory and epistemologies of (white) ignorance have shown. Allying ourselves with those already resisting daily means trusting to modes of resistance we may not ourselves be able to see—

and trusting that our students may have far better strategies for responding to reactive "back-pull" than we do.

We need to live with the uncertainties that arise from opacity, as well as from the way that, as Alexis Shotwell suggests, there is no reassuringly "pure" place from which to teach, no "preracial state we could access, erasing histories of slavery, forced labor on railroads, colonialism, genocide, and their concomitant responsibilities and requirements." Thus, "since it is not possible to avoid complicity, we do better to start from an assumption that everyone is implicated"—though not in the same way—"in situations we (at least in some way) repudiate."[38] Instead of obeying "a *moral imperative* to exclude exclusion," by seeking a speaking position unsullied by violence,[39] we do better to start by interrogating our own complicities, thereby opening spaces for others to interrogate theirs. This means learning (with Huffer) to do the patient, imperfect work of critical pedagogy on unstable ground, with no sure way to guarantee that critical gestures will not be appropriated by neoliberal agendas or, sometimes, do harm. Nonetheless, we can attend with deliberate care to relational bodies and singular existents situated within historically sedimented structures, and emphasize multiple histories of struggle and solidarity, rather than individual resilience and self-actualization.

If this kind of pedagogy points to the situatedness of both instructor and students, then rather than treating dissonance as a generalized practice—just one pedagogical strategy among many—we need instead a perspectival and distributed approach,[40] capable of attending to *who* is cultivating dissonance and *what makes it possible* for them to do so, as well as to the specific networks of relations that enable dissonance to make itself felt and condition how it works, on and for whom, at whose expense, and with what effects. Such a perspectivalism would see our speaking positions not as the site of freely chosen viewpoints but as the embodied product of a contestation of values,[41] and then undertake the genealogical work to interrogate the value of those values. Leaning on Huffer's queer feminism, as well as the work of decolonial theorists and those attending to the "afterlife of slavery,"[42] we might continue to explore the potential of a dissonant pedagogy to restore "the ungrounding cracks and instabilities that open up possibilities for transformed relations between subjects and others."[43]

And, finally, we might seek to do something I would tentatively describe as inserting a gap to allow for a lateral movement. By opening up an imaginative gap between our bodies and the conceptual, historical, material structures that capture them, we might be better able to think about our (multiple, differing) positions in relation to those structures without wholly identifying ourselves with them, creating spaces for dis-identification and change. One way of doing this might be to seek out images or texts that allow a class (including the instructor) to engage with a situation that relates to their own, but that in some materially irreducible way—due to the contingencies of birth—is not their own, and not fully imaginable *through* their own.

Encountering structures of oppression in other times and places can provide the necessary mediation that helps us more fully see the ways those structures are replicated in our own times, to secure (or erase) our own "place." Where we are too deeply (which is to say, mostly unconsciously) resistant to confronting our own complicities directly, such encounters might allow for the discomforting jolt of recognition that can be required to shift our perspective, making us more legible to ourselves, while also allowing enough distance for us to ask what work *we* need to do if violence and injustice are not to be repeated and we are not to perpetuate complicity. Perhaps, too, such imaginative encounters might offer those who endure structural injustice in the present an expanded language through which to articulate oppression and a sense of cross-cultural, cross-temporal solidarity, without making them the sole representative or access point to the experience of oppression.

Christina Sharpe provides an inspiring model of the approach I have in mind in her account of teaching the genocides of the Nazi concentration camps and of the Middle Passage alongside one another. By reversing the chronological order and teaching about the camps first, and then looping back from readings about North American slavery to Claude Lanzmann's *Shoah*, Sharpe asks her students if they can imagine,

> if, after the war's end, Simon Srebnik [one of only a few survivors of the massacre at Chelmno] had no place to go other than to return to this country and this town; to these people who would have also seen him dead; who had, in fact, tried to kill him and every other Jewish person in Chelmno. That is, I say, the condition in the post-Civil War United States of the formerly enslaved and their descendants.[44]

While Sharpe herself might not describe it like this, I would see her as performing with enormous care a dissonant pedagogy. The telling of this story in both her book and her classroom allows for a jolt of recognition that, while it may be shared, also differs according to our place in the afterlives of slavery that structure the present. Such pedagogical gestures, as Sharpe shows, are unavoidably risky: there are no guarantees they will work, or work as we might hope.

But, through her example, I am returned to the thought that the risk is worth taking—with care—when what is at stake is "our own capacities to read, think, and imagine otherwise."[45] To borrow from Shotwell, the pedagogical gestures through which we seek to do this are always "partial, finite, [in/]adequate, modest, limited—and yet worth working on, with and for."[46]

NOTES

1. References to "we" and "us" throughout this chapter refer to "those of us" who seek to teach in ways that foster this kind of transformative unlearning, recognizing that this commitment binds us together across many kinds of difference and that such differences affect how a dissonant pedagogy may be practised and inhabited.

2. On institutional defensiveness to dissonant pedagogy, see Alyssa Niccolini, "Animate Affects: Censorship, Reckless Pedagogies and Beautiful Feelings," *Gender and Education* 28.2 (2016).

3. Ada S. Jaarsma, *Kierkegaard after the Genome* (London and New York: Palgrave Macmillan, 2017), 153–54.

4. These examples are variants of classroom experiences I have had, or that others have shared with me, rather than direct representations of any particular instance.

5. bell hooks, *Teaching Community: A Pedagogy of Hope* (New York: Routledge, 2003), 36, 64.

6. Adriana Cavarero, *Inclinations: A Critique of Rectitude*, trans. Amanda Minervini and Adam Sitze (Stanford: Stanford University Press, 2016).

7. Erinn Gilson, "Vulnerability, Ignorance, and Oppression," *Hypatia* 26.2 (2011).

8. Charles Mills, "White Ignorance," and Linda Martin Alcoff, "Epistemologies of Ignorance: Three Types," in *Race and Epistemologies of Ignorance*, ed. Shannon Sullivan and Nancy Tuana (New York: SUNY Press, 2007).

9. Judith Butler, *Notes toward a Performative Theory of Assembly* (Cambridge, MA: Harvard University Press, 2015), 20–22, 66–68.

10. Achille Mbembe, *Critique of Black Reason*, trans. Laurent Dubois (Durham, NC: Duke University Press, 2017).

11. Simone de Beauvoir, *The Ethics of Ambiguity*, trans. Bernard Frechtman (New York: Citadel, 1948), 45–53.

12. Hannah Arendt, *Life of the Mind*, vol. 1, *Thinking* (New York: Harcourt, 1971), 173–75.

13. Jaarsma, *Kierkegaard after the Genome*, 154.

14. On this point, see bell hooks, *Teaching to Transgress* (New York: Routledge, 1994), 42.

15. See Christina Sharpe's similar concern with "the traumatizing and retraumatizing of Black children for the education of others" in *In the Wake: On Blackness and Being* (Durham, NC: Duke University Press, 2016), 92.

16. Gayatri Chakravorty Spivak, "Can the Subaltern Speak?" *Wedge* 7/8 (Winter/Spring 1985); *A Critique of Postcolonial Reason* (Cambridge, MA: Harvard University Press, 1999); hooks, *Teaching to Transgress*, 43–44.

17. Marilyn Frye, "Oppression," in *The Politics of Reality* (Trumansburg, NY: Crossing Press, 1983).

18. I borrow this figure from Johanna Oksala's insightful critical analysis of the neoliberal subject in *Foucault, Politics, and Violence* (Evanston, IL: Northwestern University Press, 2012), 146.

19. de Beauvoir, *The Ethics of Ambiguity*, 81–91.

20. Frantz Fanon, *Black Skin, White Masks*, trans. Richard Philcox (New York: Grove Press, 2008), 92.

21. Édouard Glissant, "For Opacity," in *Poetics of Relation*, trans. Betsy Wing (Ann Arbor: University of Michigan Press, 1997).

22. Michel Foucault, *The Order of Things* (London: Routledge, 2002).

23. In addition to Alcoff and Mills, see Sandra Harding, ed., *The Feminist Standpoint Theory Reader* (London: Routledge, 2004); Chandra Mohanty, *Feminism without Borders* (Durham, NC: Duke University Press, 2003).

24. Sheila Macrine, "What Is Critical Pedagogy Good For? An Interview with Ira Shor," in *Critical Pedagogy in Uncertain Times: Hope and Possibilities*, ed. Sheila Macrine (London and New York: Palgrave Macmillan, 2009), 134.

25. Sylvia Wynter and Greg Thomas, "Inter/Views: Sylvia Wynter," *Proud Flesh: New Afrikan Journal of Culture, Politics and Consciousness* 4 (2006): 6, 10.

26. Lynne Huffer, *Are the Lips a Grave?* (New York: Columbia University Press, 2013), 25.

27. Huffer, 20, 7.

28. Huffer, 8.

29. On the emergence of this paradigm, see Susan Bordo, *The Flight to Objectivity* (New York: SUNY Press, 1987); for an exploration of its afterlives, particularly in a pedagogical context, see Jaarsma, *Kierkegaard after the Genome*, chapter 5.

30. I agree with Shadee Malaklou that they are not. See "An Open Letter to Duke University's Class of 2007, About Your Open Letter to Stephen Miller by M. Shadee Malaklou," *The Black Scholar: Journal of Black Studies and Research*, April 5, 2017, http://www.theblackscholar.org/open-letter-duke-universitys-class-2007-open-letter-stephen-miller-m-shadee-malaklou/.

31. Macrine, "What Is Critical Pedagogy Good for?" 134.

32. Huffer, *Are the Lips a Grave?* 12.

33. Huffer, 8, 12.

34. Friedrich Nietzsche, preface to "On the Genealogy of Morals," in *Basic Writings of Nietzsche*, trans. Walter Kaufmann (New York: Random House, 2000), §1, 451; translation modified.

35. Michel Foucault, "The Return of Morality," in *Michel Foucault: Politics, Philosophy, Culture*, ed. Lawrence Kritzman (New York: Routledge, 1988), 253–54.

36. Claudia Rankine and Beth Loffreda, introduction to *The Racial Imaginary: Writers on Race in the Life of the Mind*, ed. Claudia Rankine, Beth Loffreda, and Max King Cap (Albany, NY: Fence Books, 2015), 13–14.

37. Saidiya Hartman, "Venus in Two Acts," *Small Axe* 12.2, no. 26 (2008); Katherine McKittrick, "Mathematics Black Life," *The Black Scholar: Journal of Black Studies and Research* 44.2 (2015).

38. Alexis Shotwell, *Against Purity: Living Ethically in Compromised Times* (Minneapolis: University of Minnesota Press, 2016), 4–5.

39. Huffer, *Are the Lips a Grave?* 19.

40. See Jane Bennett, *Vibrant Matter* (Durham, NC: Duke University Press, 2010), chapter 2.

41. See Sarah Kofman on Nietzschean perspectivalism in "Baubô: Theological Perversion and Fetishism," in *Nietzsche's New Seas*, ed. Michael Allen Gillespie and Tracy B. Strong (Chicago: University of Chicago Press, 1988). On perspectivalism as permitting the affirmation of incommensurable differences and divergent becomings, see Jaarsma, *Kierkegaard after the Genome,* chapter 6.

42. Saidiya Hartman, *Lose Your Mother: A Journey along the Atlantic Slave Route* (New York: Farrar, Straus and Giroux, 2007), 6.

43. Huffer, *Are the Lips a Grave?* 13.

44. Sharpe, *In the Wake*, 12.

45. Sharpe, 13.

46. Shotwell, *Against Purity*, 5.

WORKS CITED

Alcoff, Linda Martin. "Epistemologies of Ignorance: Three Types." In *Race and Epistemologies of Ignorance*, edited by Shannon Sullivan and Nancy Tuana, 39–57. New York: SUNY Press, 2007.

Arendt, Hannah. *Life of the Mind*. Vol. 1, *Thinking*. New York: Harcourt, 1971.

Bennett, Jane. *Vibrant Matter*. Durham, NC: Duke University Press, 2010.

Bordo, Susan. *The Flight to Objectivity*. New York: SUNY Press, 1987.

Butler, Judith. *Notes toward a Performative Theory of Assembly*. Cambridge, MA: Harvard University Press, 2015.

Cavarero, Adriana. *Inclinations: A Critique of Rectitude.* Translated by Amanda Minervini and Adam Sitze. Stanford: Stanford University Press, 2016.

de Beauvoir, Simone. *The Ethics of Ambiguity*. Translated by Bernard Frechtman. New York: Citadel, 1948.

Fanon, Frantz. *Black Skin, White Masks*. Translated by Richard Philcox. New York: Grove Press, 2008.

Foucault, Michel. *The Order of Things*. London: Routledge, 2002.

———. "The Return of Morality." In *Michel Foucault: Politics, Philosophy, Culture*, edited by Lawrence Kritzman, 242–54. New York: Routledge, 1988.

Frye, Marilyn. "Oppression." In *The Politics of Reality*, 1–16. Trumansburg, NY: Crossing Press, 1983.

Gilson, Erinn. "Vulnerability, Ignorance, and Oppression." *Hypatia* 26.2 (2011): 308–32.

Glissant, Édouard. "For Opacity." In *Poetics of Relation*, translated by Betsy Wing, 189–94. Ann Arbor: University of Michigan Press, 1997.

Harding, Sandra, ed. *The Feminist Standpoint Theory Reader*. London: Routledge, 2004.

Hartman, Saidiya. *Lose Your Mother: A Journey along the Atlantic Slave Route*. New York: Farrar, Straus and Giroux, 2007.

———. "Venus in Two Acts." *Small Axe* 12.2, no. 26 (2008): 1–14.

hooks, bell. *Teaching Community: A Pedagogy of Hope*. New York: Routledge, 2003.

———. *Teaching to Transgress*. New York: Routledge, 1994.

Huffer, Lynne. *Are the Lips a Grave?* New York: Columbia University Press, 2013.

Jaarsma, Ada. S. *Kierkegaard after the Genome: Science, Existence and Belief in This World*. London and New York: Palgrave Macmillan, 2017.

Kofman, Sarah. "Baubô: Theological Perversion and Fetishism." In *Nietzsche's New Seas*, edited by Michael Allen Gillespie and Tracy B. Strong, 175–202. Chicago: University of Chicago Press, 1988.

Macrine, Sheila. "What Is Critical Pedagogy Good For? An Interview with Ira Shor." In *Critical Pedagogy in Uncertain Times: Hope and Possibilities*, edited by Sheila Macrine, 119–36. London and New York: Palgrave Macmillan, 2009.

Malaklou, Shadee. "An Open Letter to Duke University's Class of 2007, About Your Open Letter to Stephen Miller By M. Shadee Malaklou." *The Black Scholar: Journal of Black Studies and Research*, April 5, 2017. http://www.theblackscholar.org/open-letter-duke-universitys-class-2007-open-letter-stephen-miller-m-shadee-malaklou/.

Mbembe, Achille. *Critique of Black Reason*. Translated by Laurent Dubois. Durham, NC: Duke University Press, 2017.

McKittrick, Katherine. "Mathematics Black Life." *The Black Scholar: Journal of Black Studies and Research* 44.2 (2015): 16–28.

Mills, Charles. "White Ignorance." In *Race and Epistemologies of Ignorance*, edited by Shannon Sullivan and Nancy Tuana, 13–38. New York: SUNY Press, 2007.

Mohanty, Chandra. *Feminism without Borders*. Durham, NC: Duke University Press, 2003.

Niccolini, Alyssa. "Animate Affects: Censorship, Reckless Pedagogies and Beautiful Feelings." *Gender and Education* 28.2 (2016): 230–49.

Nietzsche, Friedrich. Preface to "On the Genealogy of Morals." In *Basic Writings of Nietzsche*, translated by W. Kaufmann, 451–59. New York: Random House, 2000.

Oksala, Johanna. *Foucault, Politics, and Violence*. Evanston, IL: Northwestern University Press, 2012.

Rankine, Claudia, and Beth Loffreda. Introduction to *The Racial Imaginary: Writers on Race in the Life of the Mind*, edited by Claudia Rankine, Beth Loffreda, and Max King Cap, 13–22. Albany, NY: Fence Books, 2015.

Sharpe, Christina. *In the Wake: On Blackness and Being*. Durham, NC: Duke University Press, 2016.

Shotwell, Alexis. *Against Purity: Living Ethically in Compromised Times*. Minneapolis: University of Minnesota Press, 2016.

Spivak, Gayatri Chakravorty. "Can the Subaltern Speak?" *Wedge* 7/8 (Winter/Spring 1985): 120–30.

———. *A Critique of Postcolonial Reason*. Cambridge, MA: Harvard University Press, 1999.

Wynter, Sylvia, and Greg Thomas. "Inter/Views: Sylvia Wynter." *Proud Flesh: New Afrikan Journal of Culture, Politics and Consciousness* 4 (2006): 1–36.

Afterword

KIT DOBSON

DISSONANT METHODS EMERGED AT A PARTICULAR MOMENT and in response to particular pressures. Within the university system—both in North America, in which this book's conversations are situated, and well beyond—pressures to realign pedagogy, the classroom itself, as well as research agendas, with narrowly conceived utilitarian aims have struck me as increasingly hindering the sorts of academic labour that my peers and I have attempted to undertake. The labour of thought—as well as its affective registers—is difficult to describe in advance, yet universities have been turning to "outcome"-focused teaching as a way to attempt to speak to impoverished public funding bodies, as well as to external, private funders—whose funds have become more important than ever in a time of dwindling public support. Research funders, too, increasingly appeared to be turning to this model (as I have written about elsewhere[1]). I felt, I will admit, some amount of despair at the situation, and I knew, from many conversations, that I was far from alone in my concerns about what amounts to a long-running trend.

Was there any possibility for action in this climate? The first editor and prime mover of this collection, Ada Jaarsma, felt there was—and even that despair might motivate that action—and she must take the lion's share of credit for what successes this volume might have. Turning to the recently established pedagogical subfield of the Scholarship of Teaching and Learning (SoTL), which seeks to understand pedagogy through a variety of measures, many of them quantitative, but some, as well, qualitative in nature, she determined that we might propose an intervention.[2] After securing support from our own institution's Institute for SoTL, we were able to organize and mount the initial workshop in Banff that led to this present volume.

This book, however, builds on much more than SoTL scholarship, for we sought to find contributors whose qualitative and experiential thinking would lead to a rich conversation or dialogue across the disciplinary forms of what is variously known as the arts, the humanities, or *les sciences humaines*. We were very consciously building on edited collections such as *Not Drowning but Waving: Women, Feminism and the Liberal Arts*, edited by Susan Brown, Jeanne Perreault, Jo-Ann Wallace, and Heather Zwicker, in its considerations of gender in the academy, as well *Retooling the Humanities: The Culture of Research in Canadian Universities*, edited by Daniel Coleman and Smaro Kamboureli.[3] We were also very conscious of recent writing about the place of the arts in the academy, particularly books like Martha Nussbaum's *Not for Profit: Why Democracy Needs the Humanities* and Maggie Berg and Barbara Seeber's widely discussed book, *The Slow Professor: Challenging the Culture of Speed in the Academy*.[4] That last book, in its plea for faculty to take on elements of the slow movement in order to interrupt the university's economic rationalizations for ever-increasing speed (and as a result disparity), is, in my view, crucial, even if it does not tell the whole story.

I have been revitalized in my own pedagogical thinking by the project that became *Dissonant Methods*, additionally, because of the ways in which academic disciplines have the ability to become so very disciplinary—in the sense that Foucault and his inheritors might think of the term. That is, academic disciplines may govern thinking processes more than I have been accustomed to acknowledge. My home discipline of English is, as I write, undergoing a change, a metamorphosis into something new. Many colleagues, when I speak with them, are no longer certain of the discipline's shape, and neither am I. Is it a discipline determined by its historical periods? Do all English majors need to take a course on Shakespeare, for instance? Is the discipline about genre? Is it about national literatures? Or about the medium? What of cultural studies, film studies, creative writing? How do these relate to English? Is English a language or something having to do with literature? That I can ask these questions means that, to some extent, I have a pre-existing understanding of English as a discipline—and it means that, in turn, my own thinking has been shaped, or disciplined, by the discipline itself. I am, by nature, suspicious of being disciplined; I take one cue from Foucault and his cautions in, above all else, *Discipline and Punish* about the nature of Western societies that, in his view from at least the eighteenth century onward, have sought to inculcate modes of social discipline and self-discipline into the quotidian operations of their citizens.[5]

How, then, are disciplines disciplinary? And how might those disciplinary norms be challenged or undone? What are the methods that might be used in order to achieve such a challenge or undoing? In *Death of a Discipline*, Gayatri Spivak calls for the rebirth of the discipline of comparative literature through its death. She notes along the way that there are "many institutional obstacles" to change and to cross-disciplinary collaboration, one of which she terms "disciplinary fear."[6] *Dissonant Methods* is one set of potential, provisional answers to those questions, or a possible series of solutions to the "disciplinary fear" that Spivak invokes. When the three clusters of this book emerged—around the event, embodiment, and the political—I began better to understand how some of the anxieties that fed into the creation of this project could be addressed. The insistence on the evental nature of pedagogy—on the things that happen in the classroom that emerge, the unforeseen events that are, after all, the crux of pedagogy—runs throughout the volume. At the moment of the event, perhaps, we find learning that pushes back against narrow conceptions of the purpose of education and research—these are the moments in which the classroom and learning become undisciplined, in the best sense possible of the term. Such moments are not dissimilar to the joy that one might find in having one's research suddenly turn in a new, unexpected direction because of a fortuitous finding (which is, after all, how many key shifts in thinking happen, across the disciplines).

The moment of the event, in turn, becomes an embodied moment. Because it has not been—cannot have been, by definition—planned in advance, what happens in the event varies. Its impacts are embodied ones, ones where performance, performativity, and the fleshy matter of which bodies are made intersect. Yet learning, as this book argues, is not simply a matter of separating mind and body—and neither is it simply one of bringing them together. Instead, the state of embodiment that pedagogy finds itself working through is con-siderably messier, always contingent, and always in process. The classroom might be said to be the result of what happens when embodied, fleshy beings come together in order to pursue a set of linked questions. Their imperfections and flaws may come out in myriad ways, as might their brilliance and insight; indeed, these categories may all be linked and be the key to what provisional answers might be found along the way.

The embodied event, in turn, is by its nature political. Politics, as they emerge across this volume, can hinge on many things: politics with a capital *P*, but also the ways in which the classroom turns on how the *polis* comes together in order to negotiate with itself. Those political moments are those where the body inspires thinking, ones where thought can take place. Events are political; embodied beings are political; understanding the ways in which events and bodies intersect, too, is highly political in nature.

The event, embodiment, and the political emerged in this volume very much by chance. As editors, Ada Jaarsma and I did not set out to organize a volume along these lines from the beginning. Rather, our intention at the outset was to assemble thinkers who work in a wide mix of humanities disciplines and who also take pedagogy to reside at the heart of their thinking. At this stage, it is gratifying to see the book's three threads emerge, as they are very fertile ones for further thinking. The classroom, that vexed space, remains, as bell hooks put it, "the most radical space of possibility in the academy."[7] Or, as Gert Biesta puts it, against a utilitarian world often more interested in what he terms "learnification" than genuine engagement,[8] it remains possible for pedagogical endeavours to remain transformative ones, ones where, against the odds (and against ever-enlarging classrooms and ever-increasing pressures on students), critical engagement can take place.

NOTES

1. See my essay, "Mining the Valley of Its Making: Culture and Knowledge as Market Commodities in Humanities Research," in *Retooling the Humanities: The Culture of Research in Canadian Universities*, ed. Daniel Coleman and Smaro Kamboureli (Edmonton: University of Alberta Press, 2011).

2. On Ada Jaarsma's scholarship in this area, see "On Being Taught," *The Canadian Journal for the Scholarship of Teaching and Learning* 6.2 (2016). I am also, however, thinking of her chapter "Tomatoes in the Classroom" in *Kierkegaard after the Genome: Science, Existence and Belief in this World* (London and New York: Palgrave MacMillan, 2017).

3. Susan Brown et al., eds., *Not Drowning but Waving: Women, Feminism and the Liberal Arts* (Edmonton: University of Alberta Press, 2011); Daniel Coleman and Smaro Kamboureli, eds., *Retooling the Humanities: The Culture of Research in Canadian Universities* (Edmonton: University of Alberta Press, 2011).

4. Martha Nussbaum, *Not for Profit: Why Democracy Needs the Humanities* (Princeton: Princeton University Press, 2011); Maggie Berg and Barbara Seeber, *The Slow Professor: Challenging the Culture of Speed in the Academy* (Toronto: University of Toronto Press, 2016).

5. While this brief afterword is not the space to discuss Michel Foucault's thinking on disciplinarity in depth, it seems worth taking a moment to acknowledge the ways in which his analysis of a shift in Western society from a society of confession toward a society of discipline might help thinking to grapple with the contemporary moment. Society may be in the midst of shifting anew, moreover, and the directions that it takes will surely tell its participants a great deal about themselves. In addition to *Discipline and Punish: The Birth of the Prison*, trans. Alan Sheridan (New York: Vintage, 1995), it is also important to highlight the lectures that Foucault was delivering around the same time, which have been published in several volumes. Particularly useful to my own thinking is the volume *"Society Must Be Defended": Lectures at the Collège de France, 1975–1976*, trans. David Macey (New York: Picador, 2003).

6. Gayatri Chakravorty Spivak, *Death of a Discipline* (New York: Columbia University Press, 2003), 19.

7. bell hooks, *Teaching to Transgress: Education as the Practice of Freedom* (New York: Routledge, 1994), 12.

8. See Gert Biesta, *The Beautiful Risk of Education* (New York: Routledge, 2014).

WORKS CITED

Berg, Maggie, and Barbara Seeber. *The Slow Professor: Challenging the Culture of Speed in the Academy*. Toronto: University of Toronto Press, 2016.

Biesta, Gert. *The Beautiful Risk of Education*. New York: Routledge, 2014.

Brown, Susan, Jeanne Perreault, Jo-Ann Wallace, and Heather Zwicker, eds. *Not Drowning but Waving: Women, Feminism and the Liberal Arts*. Edmonton: University of Alberta Press, 2011.

Coleman, Daniel, and Smaro Kamboureli, eds. *Retooling the Humanities: The Culture of Research in Canadian Universities*. Edmonton: University of Alberta Press, 2011.

Dobson, Kit. "Mining the Valley of Its Making: Culture and Knowledge as Market Commodities in Humanities Research." In *Retooling the Humanities: The Culture of Research in Canadian Universities*, edited by Daniel Coleman and Smaro Kamboureli, 77–93. Edmonton: University of Alberta Press, 2011.

Foucault, Michel. *Discipline and Punish: The Birth of the Prison*. Translated by Alan Sheridan. New York: Vintage, 1995.

———. *"Society Must Be Defended": Lectures at the Collège de France, 1975–1976*. Translated by David Macey. New York: Picador, 2003.

hooks, bell. *Teaching to Transgress: Education as the Practice of Freedom*. New York: Routledge, 1994.

Jaarsma, Ada S. *Kierkegaard after the Genome: Science, Existence and Belief in This World*. London and New York: Palgrave MacMillan, 2017.

———. "On Being Taught." *The Canadian Journal for the Scholarship of Teaching and Learning* 6.2 (2016): 1–12.

Nussbaum, Martha. *Not for Profit: Why Democracy Needs the Humanities*. Princeton: Princeton University Press, 2011.

Spivak, Gayatri Chakravorty. *Death of a Discipline*. New York: Columbia University Press, 2003.

Contributors

Kathy Cawsey is an associate professor at Dalhousie University in Halifax. She is the author of *Twentieth-Century Chaucer Criticism: Reading Audiences* (Ashgate, 2011) and teaches Chaucer, Middle English literature, Old English literature, Arthurian literature, and J.R.R. Tolkien. She has published on pedagogy, Middle English literature, and modern fantasy literature.

Kit Dobson is a professor of English at Mount Royal University in Calgary. He is, most recently, the author of *Malled: Deciphering Shopping in Canada* (Wolsak & Wynn, 2017). Past books include *Transnational Canadas: Anglo-Canadian Literature and Globalization* (Wilfrid Laurier University Press, 2009), and, co-edited with Áine McGlynn, *Transnationalism, Activism, Art* (University of Toronto Press, 2013). His teaching focuses on literatures in Canada, Indigenous literatures, writing, and film.

Ada S. Jaarsma is a professor of philosophy at Mount Royal University in Calgary. She is the author of *Kierkegaard after the Genome* (Palgrave Macmillan, 2017), and works at the intersections of continental philosophy, critical disability studies, Scholarship of Teaching and Learning, and science studies. She is interested in phenomena like placebos and epigenetics that demonstrate the entangled relations between biology and social life, as well as the porous lines between what heals and what harms.

Rachel Jones is Associate Professor in Philosophy and Affiliate Faculty in Women and Gender Studies at George Mason University, Virginia. She is the author of *Irigaray* (Polity, 2011) and works on Kant and post-Kantian European philosophy as read through feminist, queer, decolonial, and critical race perspectives. She is interested in contested subjects and resistant objects, and relational ontologies that attend to bodily difference, plural singularity, birth and natality, and human and more-than-human materialities.

Kyle Kinaschuk is a poet and scholar. He is a doctoral candidate in the Department of English at the University of Toronto, where he researches Canadian literature and criticism, poetry and poetics, critical theory, and the philosophy and theory of pedagogy. He is the author of a chapbook, *COLLECTIONS-14* (above/ground press, 2019). His poetry and writing have appeared in the *Capilano Review*, *PRISM international*, *Canadian Literature*, and elsewhere.

Namrata Mitra is an assistant professor of English at Iona College, New York. She earned a Ph.D. in philosophy and literature at Purdue University, Indiana, in 2012. She has published articles and book chapters on comparative postcolonial theories, unrecognizability of routine sexual violence in South Asia, and the problem of unacknowledged contexts in philosophical argumentation. In addition to instructing core classes in English and philosophy, she teaches courses in feminist literature and postcolonial studies.

Guy Obrecht attended the National Ballet School of Canada before turning to music studies at the Conservatory of Music in Gatineau, Quebec. His undergraduate degree at the University of Ottawa included studies in music composition and theory. He went on to complete a master's degree in music theory from the University of Toronto and a Ph.D. in music from the University of California, San Diego. He is currently a senior lecturer at Mount Royal University in Calgary where he teaches music and aesthetics courses in the context of the liberal arts.

Katja K. Pettinen teaches cultural anthropology, linguistics, and science studies at Mount Royal University in Calgary. She has a Ph.D. in anthropology from Purdue University, Indiana, and is the founder of Bujinkan Calgary Dojo, which teaches traditional Japanese martial arts. She researches and publishes in feminist science studies and anthropology.

Kaitlin Rothberger is a Ph.D. student at McMaster University where she majors in English and cultural studies. Her research interests include the epistemological significance of communal walking, critical pedagogy, and disability studies. She participated in the Banff Centre workshop on "Dissonant Methods" as a research assistant.

Ely Shipley is the author of *Some Animal* (Nightboat, 2018), *Boy with Flowers* (Barrow Street, 2008), and *On Beards: A Memoir of Passing*, a letterpress chapbook (speCt! Books, 2016). He taught for many years at Baruch College, City University of New York, and is currently an assistant professor at Western Washington University in Bellingham.

Martin Shuster is a philosopher who teaches at Goucher College in Baltimore, Maryland, where he is jointly appointed in the Center for Geographies of Justice and the Center for Humanities. In addition to many articles and essays in various areas of philosophy, he is the author of *Autonomy after Auschwitz: Adorno, German Idealism and Modernity* and *New Television: The Aesthetics and Politics of a Genre*, both published by University of Chicago Press, 2014 and 2017, respectively.

Index

Athabasca University Press | aupress.ca

Regime of Obstruction

How Corporate Power Blocks Energy Democracy

Edited by William K. Carroll

978–1–77199–289–3 (paperback)

The Medium Is the Monster

Canadian Adaptations of Frankenstein and the Discourse of Technology

Mark A. McCutcheon

978–1–77199–236–7 (hardcover)

978–1–77199–224–4 (paperback)

Public Deliberation on Climate Change

Lessons from Alberta Climate Dialogue

Edited by Lorelei L. Hanson

978–1–77199–215–2 (paperback)

University of Alberta Press | uap.ualberta.ca

Dissonant Methods

Undoing Discipline in the Humanities Classroom

Ada S. Jaarsma and Kit Dobson, Editors

978–1–77212–489–7 (paperback)

Feminist Acts

Branching Out *Magazine and the Making of Canadian Feminism*

Tessa Jordan

978–1–77212–484–2 (paperback)

Keetsahnak / Our Missing and Murdered Indigenous Sisters

Kim Anderson, Maria Campbell, and Christi Belcourt, Editors

978–1–77212–367–8 (paperback)

University of Calgary Press | press.ucalgary.ca

Creating the Future of Health

The History of the Cumming School of Medicine at the University of Calgary, 1967–2012

Robert Lampard, David B. Hogan, Frank W. Stahnisch, and James R. Wright Jr.

978–1–77385–164–8 (paperback)

Intertwined Histories

Plants in Their Social Contexts

Edited by Jim Ellis

978–1–77385–090–0 (paperback)

Water Rites

Reimagining Water in the West

Edited by Jim Ellis

978–1–55238–997–3 (paperback)